THE MINUTIAE OF THE MEETING

Essays on Quaker Connections

Max L. Carter

GUILFORD COLLEGE
5800 West Friendly Avenue, Greensboro, NC 27410
1999

ISBN 0-9674045-0-9

Cover: The famous iron bridge across England's Severn River.

This bridge, built in 1779 by Quaker iron master Abraham Darby III, is the world's first cast iron span. This picture is chosen for the cover, not to imply most of these essays are "fabricated," too, but to symbolize the "bridges" they form connecting Friends to the wider society.

Manufactured in the United States of America
Composed by Friendly Desktop Publishing
Printed by Thomson–Shore

Dedication

This collection of essays is dedicated to the nearly one hundred students who have graduated from, or are currently in, the Quaker Leadership Scholars Program (QLSP) at Guilford College. Their enthusiasm for the Religious Society of Friends is contagious and gives me enormous hope for the future of the Quaker movement.

Proceeds from the sale of this book go to support QLSP, campus ministry, and other programs of Friends Center at Guilford College.

Contents

Introduction

This collection of brief essays is a primarily light–hearted look at some of the *minutiae* of Quaker history. No heavy theology here; just leaden puns and wordplays! That said, it is also not intended to be merely another list of "Friendly trivia." Oddities of Quaker history and social contributions are presented within some broader context and with a little "fleshing out."

The basic premise of the collection is this: items and "trivia" are selected only upon mention in some way in the popular media of radio, TV, newspapers, or magazines. In some cases, the Quaker connection is made apparent in the original source. In others, a connection has to be made—and sometimes quite tenuously! But we are not shamefaced in these pages about making even the most obscure connection with Friends! It does mean, however, that this is no exhaustive (if exhausting) survey of Quaker history! Instead of "All the news that's fit to print," this collection is merely, "All the news that *fits*, we print."

These essays had their birth in brief notices in the weekly memos to students at Guilford College, Greensboro, North Carolina, who are in the Quaker Leadership Scholars Program (QLSP). Each weekly memo for several years in the 1990s began with a "Quaker Trivia" lead–in. These items were expanded and added to during a sabbatical in England during the 1998–99 academic year. This will help explain the preponderance of Greensboro and English media sources, as well as the occasional odd spellings of words! But I hope this peculiarly mixed "flavour" will find your favor.

I am grateful to the QLSP students who put up with these weekly "groaners," and to Woodbrooke Quaker Centre in Birmingham, England, for providing a Friend–in–Residence position during spring term 1999. Utilization of Woodbrooke's excellent library, daily newspapers, and a captive audience on which to try some of these essays was key to completing this collection.

Special thanks go to Gertrude Beal and B. J. Weatherby for expert editing and friendly encouragement.

Of course, I also thank Guilford College for providing the context out of which the original seed grew and for offering the sabbatical leave. They were probably just glad to be rid of me for a year!

Effort has been made, in spite of the "scholarship lite" nature of these essays, to be as accurate as possible with facts and figures. Where appropriate, sources are suggested for further reading on a subject. Finding fault in other Friends' historical interpretations is a cottage industry among Quakers, though, and I certainly expect to be taken aside by numerous people who take issue with my tongue–in–cheek presentations here. This does not excuse mistakes in facts, however, and for those I take responsibility and welcome correction. The same holds for the illustrations in this collection, all drawn from slides I have accummulated over the years. I apologize for any offense caused to those who have a better photographic eye than I!

An ancestor of mine was a "public Friend," often traveling "on a minute" from his Quaker meeting. These travels took him away from home for long stretches of time, and his absences became the stuff of family lore. One of the stories handed down through the years is of his wife's asking him to do some chore around the house, to which he responded, "I'll get around to it in a minute." His wife replied, "Is that a Quaker minute, dear?"

I hope these Quaker minutiae are not found to be too long, or too much of a chore.

Six degrees of Quakerism

They used to swallow goldfish or stuff dozens in the old Volkswagen "Beetle," but now college students are getting more cerebral. According to the 30 September 1996 *Newsweek*, three college students in 1993 dreamed up a game called "Six degrees of Kevin Bacon." The idea of the game is to try to link any actor or actress with Hollywood star Kevin Bacon by building a chain of films with common figures in their casts.

Heck! Any Quaker can play such a name game with other Friends and find a mutual relationship in far fewer than six moves!

What the *Newsweek* article failed to do was play that game with Bacon's own association with Quakers, possibly because it would have taken only one move!

The popular actor's father is Edmund Bacon, a Philadelphia Friend and acclaimed city planner responsible for many features of the Quaker City's urban landscape. It was Bacon who carried out Philadelphia's massive Center City re–development project in the 1950s; he succeeded in bringing the city into the twentieth century but left untouched founder William Penn's grid pattern and large public squares.

Less successfully, Bacon developed the area around historic Independence Hall — creating the Independence Mall National Park. Even he laments now the wholesale destruction of several city blocks of buildings to form a rather sterile mall stretching from the site of the signing of the Declaration of Independence to the Benjamin Franklin Bridge. He is currently working on new plans to make the mall more "user friendly."

Left untouched by the original project was the Philadelphia "Free" Quaker Meeting House, still standing on the east side of the mall. Built by Philadelphia's Revolutionary War era "fighting Friends" who left the main body of Quakers or were disowned for their support for the war, the meetinghouse served the splinter group until the last members died in the 1830s.

Among the attenders of the meeting was the Philadelphia Quaker Elizabeth Claypoole, better known to history as Betsy Ross. Her old spirit is probably kept in stitches by the city's flagging zeal for the barren landscape wrought by fellow Friend Edmund Bacon! It probably raises her temperature a few *degrees*.

• • •

For further reading: Robert H. Wilson, ed., *Philadelphia Quakers 1681–1981* (Philadelphia Yearly Meeting Committee for Publication, 1981).

"Free" Quaker Meeting House on Philadelphia's Independence Mall

Rich Friends and interesting characters

The 27 April 1997 *News & Record* of Greensboro, North Carolina, supplied the Quaker trivia mill with considerable grist. In that issue the book *The Wealthy 100* was reviewed and mention was made of Henrietta Howland Robinson Green (1834–1916), an eccentric Quaker–born millionaire whose penury was legendary.

The Howlands were a wealthy New York Quaker family whose largesse (before Henrietta!) enabled New Garden Boarding School (predecessor to Guilford College) to open in 1837. North Carolina patriarch Nathan Hunt had been promised a large gift from the Howlands as soon as a shipment of goods was received and sold. Hunt reported to the yearly meeting education committee that he had a "vision" in which the boat arrived safely and the future of the boarding school project was assured. New Garden's ship finally came in!

Mary Mendenhall Hobbs, wife of Guilford's first president, attended Miss Howland's School in New York, where she became a close friend of M. Carey Thomas, later president of Quaker–founded Bryn Mawr College and niece of Quaker devotional writer Hannah Whitall Smith. Mary was also introduced at the school to the Holiness preaching of Quaker evangelist David B. Updegraff, who proclaimed her transformed. A mature M. M. Hobbs later doubted the accuracy of his pronouncement.

But this does segue—eventually—into further Quaker connections in the same issue of the *News & Record*. In an article on the national volunteer conference held in Philadelphia, the paper reported that hundreds of volunteers during the conference fanned out along Germantown Avenue to engage in service projects.

Antislavery historical marker on Germantown Avenue

Germantown Avenue gets its name from the Dutch and German Quakers and Mennonites who established Germantown, Pennsylvania, north of Philadelphia in 1683. The road follows an old Indian path and passes many noted Quaker sites: Lucretia Mott's grave in the Fairhill Burial Ground; the site of the Revolutionary War Battle of Germantown, led by disowned Quaker Nathanael Greene (after whom Greensboro, itself, is named); the Underground Railroad station of the Quaker Johnson family; and the place where, in 1688, Friends penned the Germantown Remonstrance, the first European protest against slavery in the American colonies.

Among the signers were the Op den Graeff ancestors of aforementioned Holiness preacher David B. Updegraff. I assume that the Germantown Avenue volunteers — if not the antislavery protesters — felt "holier than thou!"

• • •

For further reading: Barbour, Densmore, Moger, Sorel, Van Wagner, and Worrall, eds. *Quaker Crosscurrents, 300 Years of Friends in the New York Yearly Meetings* (Syracuse University Press, 1995).

*Johnson house on Germantown Avenue,
a Quaker station on the Underground Railroad*

Home of David B. Updegraff in Mt. Pleasant, Ohio

The flowering of Quakerism

An article about the Sarah P. Duke Gardens on the campus of Duke University in the 8 May 1999 *News & Record* gives us a choice between two Quaker connections. We could go with the fact that Duke University traces its origins to a little nineteenth century academy in Trinity, North Carolina, run jointly by Quakers and Methodists. The Quakers opted out of an offer from the Duke family to fund the expansion of the school into a college with the wealth generated by the Dukes' tobacco empire. Obviously having fewer scruples about taking "the devil's money," the Methodists developed the academy into Trinity College, eventually moving to Durham, North Carolina, where the college became Duke University in 1924.

But we are still bitter about that, so we won't go with that story! Instead, the focus of this reflection will be on one of the photographs illustrating the article: a stunning picture of a wistaria vine loaded with pendent lavender clusters.

The wistaria (also spelled wisteria) is named in honor of Caspar Wistar (1761–1818), a Philadelphia Quaker physician and author of the first American anatomy text. A German Friend, he migrated to America in 1717, followed ten years later by his brother, John, whose family name of Wüster was Anglicized differently as Wister. John's home, called "Grumblethorpe," and "Wister's Woods" still stand along Germantown Ave. It was John who actually went into business growing things, eventually becoming wealthy from selling the product of a different kind of vine: wine grapes. Heck, if the Methodists can grow colleges out of tobacco, Quakers can be indulged with a little viniculture!

Caspar Wistar is not the only Quaker with a plant named after him. The fothergillia, a shade–loving ground cover, honors the English physician John Fothergill (1712–1780). He was noted not only for his medical practice and friendship with Benjamin Franklin but also for his extensive botanical gardens.

Friends have long believed that to the observant person God is revealed as clearly in nature as in the written word, so it is no surprise that the movement has produced a number of noted physicians, apothecaries, and naturalists. George Fox himself urged the study of the nature of herbs, roots, plants, and trees in the first Quaker schools, and William Penn encouraged the same to his own children. But it is highly unlikely that the foxglove or foxtail plants are named for Fox. He stitched *britches*, and he rarely brought up the *rear*! The Penn name, however, is associated with a whole woods: Penn's *sylvania*!

Friends have, indeed, produced a bumper crop of outstanding botanists, including author Edwin Way Teale and author and TV personality Euell Gibbons, who is remembered for his Grapenuts ads. ("Ever eat a pine tree? Many parts are edible!") Space allows mention of only a few others, however, and we'll selectively thin the list to some of those who left behind well–known collections of plants.

John Bartram (1699–1777) established the first botanical garden in America; Bartram's Garden still offers visitors a green respite from the blight of the otherwise industrialized Schuylkill River shoreline in Philadelphia. His son William was also a naturalist and authored his influential *Travels* in 1791, a book that catalogued the plants of the southeastern United States.

Joshua and Samuel Peirce, Quaker farmers near Kennett Square, Pennsylvania, used their horticultural interests to develop "Peirce's Park" as an arboretum unrivalled in nineteenth century America. Their work formed the basis for the renowned Longwood Gardens, a project made possible by the wealth of Wilmington, Delaware, chemicals magnate Pierre S. duPont, who bought the Peirce family farm in 1906.

The duPonts made their money with gunpowder, almost as dubious a source of income as Duke tobacco! Perhaps this and a long list of notable Quaker botanists may give us some solace as we feel morally superior, even though they seem to have gotten the "flower," and Quakers got the "shaft!"

• • •

For further reading: Euell Gibbons, *Stalking the Wild Asparagus* (New York: D. McKay Co., 1971).

Peirce homestead at Longwood Gardens

A young Quaker "loses her head" in Longwood's topiary garden

Laboring with Friends

Reader's Digest, long a favorite source of divine inspiration for pastoral Friends, provides an interesting tidbit of Quaker trivia in the January 1996 edition. In the feature "Tales out of School," a story is related about Whites High School in Wabash, Indiana. Hanging in the school gymnasium are basketball team pictures from past years. In many of them a player is holding a basketball identifying the year— "62–63," "63–64," etc. The punch line of the story is that one day a freshman looking at the pictures commented, "Isn't it strange how the teams always lost by one point?"

It is also strange that the *Digest* did not mention that Whites High School began its life in the 1850s as a Quaker school. Josiah White, the Philadelphia Quaker founder of the Lehigh Coal and Navigation Company, left a large sum of money with Indiana Yearly Meeting to found a manual training school "for the education of poor children— irrespective of race or color." Among the intended beneficiaries of such training were Native Americans and descendants of African slaves.

With funds added to it by White's daughters, the bequest enabled the yearly meeting to purchase seven hundred acres near Wabash and erect several buildings. A similar institute was built in Iowa. Until the early 1970s, White's Institute in Indiana remained a manual labor school, with resident students alternating between two weeks' work on the school's farm and in other aspects of the school community's life, and two weeks in the classroom. Today known as White's Residential and Family Services, White's continues under the care of Friends to serve abused, neglected, and troubled youth.

Given Indiana Quakers' already well–developed academy system in the mid–1800s, Josiah White's occupation and Philadelphia Quaker paternalism, one might make the accusation that the manual labor institute proposal was an example of "carrying coals to New Castle." But that would be an unfair assessment. New Castle, Indiana, is some 60 miles south of Wabash!

• • •

For further reading: Errol T. Elliott, *Quakers on the American Frontier* (Richmond, IN: Friends United Press, 1969).

Sign to White's Institute, near Wabash, Indiana

Drugged out Quakers?

Conservative political commentator George Will wrote about America's growing drug crisis in his syndicated column appearing in the 19 September 1996 *News & Record*. In his essay, Will cites a report from the late 1700s that Nantucket ladies followed "the Asiatic custom of taking a dose of opium every morning." Now, any Quaker would take note of that, knowing that Nantucket was a thoroughly Quaker community at that time! Woman's rights advocate Lucretia Coffin Mott was born there; Quaker–founded Macy's Department Store originated there; even Starbucks Coffee is named after the coffee–swilling Nantucket Quaker sailor in Melville's *Moby Dick*.

Speaking of the Quaker recreational drug of choice—coffee—let us get back to Will's commentary on opium. In fact, Quaker use of the poppy derivative was not unheard of. In the nineteenth century, opiate products were prescribed for pain relief the way aspirin is today. Even saintly Elizabeth Fry, noted prison reformer, is known to have become addicted to laudanum, a tincture of opium, following a doctor's prescription for the pain of bearing more than a

Site of Elizabeth Fry's London home at St. Mildred's Court

19

dozen children. At the height of her addiction, Betsy Fry was up to a grain of opium a day; the normal dosage was one–quarter! But please, don't take that as license to "go thou and do likewise." She was a professional Quaker; do not try this at home.

Later in his essay, Will also mentions John Wesley and his concern for England's "gin–sodden society" of the eighteenth century. This founder of Methodism was once queried about how far his popular theological concept of free will (as opposed to Calvinist predestination) could be taken.

"Might *all* be saved?" asked an inquirer. "Even *Quakers*?" To which Wesley is reported to have replied, "We cannot presume to know the limits of God's miraculous grace."

I think Wesley must have been on drugs at the time!

• • •

For further reading: June Rose, *Elizabeth Fry* (London: Quaker Home Service, 1994).

*Statue of John Wesley in front of London's Wesley Chapel
near George Fox's burial site in Bunhill Fields*

20

There once was a
Quaker from Nantucket...

Move over Pepsi, Cheerwine, sweetened ice tea, and even one of the South's other official drinks—white lightning! According to the *News & Record* of 20 November 1996, Seattle–based coffee giant Starbucks was poised to douse the Tarheel State with another thick, black substance. Coffee is, indeed, the preferred addiction of many Friends, but the Quaker connection here is actually with the name of the Starbucks Corporation, derived, as mentioned in the previous essay, from the name of a Nantucket Quaker in *Moby Dick*.

As related in that essay, Nantucket was home to a strong Friends community, engaged primarily in whaling; many old Quaker names had long association with the island. In addition to a large Starbucks contingent, Nantucket also was home to Macys, Folgers (another coffee name), Rotches, and Coffins. Perhaps observing slavery to java madness sensitized such abolitionist heavyweights as Lucretia Coffin Mott and Levi and Catherine Coffin into carrying on their campaigns!

My personal favorite contemporary Coffin is T. Eugene Coffin, a well–respected Quaker minister who served for many years on the staff of Robert Schuler's Crystal Cathedral. His main job for the "Possibility Thinking" guru? Selling cemetery plots! Would a Coffin let you down?

But back to coffee and its addictive cousin, tea. Many early Quaker fortunes were built on the foundations of coffee and tea. Merchants, including Elizabeth Fry's husband, Joseph, developed family banks

21

Home of Levi and Catherine Coffin in Newport (Fountain City), Indiana

out of their business countinghouses. From *moving* beans they became *bean counters*!

It was two ships owned by Nantucket Quaker Rotches that carried the ill–fated cargo of tea into Boston Harbor in 1773, and the Philadelphia consignees of the tea were two Quaker firms, T & I Wharton and the appropriately named James & Drinker! As all good students of U.S. history know, the tea wound up in the harbor, tossed overboard, as legend has it, by patriots dressed as Native Americans. Just goes to show that Quaker relations with Indians weren't always good!

• • •

For further reading: Robert J. Leach and Peter Gow, *Quaker Nantucket* (Nantucket: Mill Hill Press, 1997).

Quakers came to do good — and did well!

Given the Quaker penchant for integrity, people soon learned that one can *bank* on Friends! Indeed, Friends established many notable financial institutions. Quaker countinghouses; small shops; iron, gold and silver smithing; and a reputation for honesty combined to lead such Friends as the Lloyds, Frys, Gurneys, Bevans, Backhouses, and Barclays into commercial banking. This history is recalled by two articles in the *Times* of London for 28 November 1998.

The first, about the resignation of Barclays Bank chief executive Martin Taylor, makes no mention of Barclays' Quaker origins. It does mention, however, that before joining the banking firm, Taylor had been in charge of the cotton–spinning operations of textile and chemicals conglomerate Courtaulds, where he was responsible for launching the Wonderbra! Make what you will of old Quaker culture's reputation for mutual support.

Barclays' Quaker underpinnings are mentioned, though, in an adjacent article. At the same time that Martin Taylor announced his departure, Barclays Bank was also coping with the impending retirement of its chairman, Andrew Buxton. His leaving the bank meant that, for the first time since Barclays was formed by a merger of the Gurney, Bevan, Backhouse, and Barclay banks in 1894, none of the old Quaker families would be represented on the bank's board.

Buxton's lineage goes back to the Gurney family and his ancestor Thomas Fowell Buxton's marriage in 1807 to Hannah Gurney, sister to Elizabeth Gurney Fry and Joseph John Gurney. Fowell Buxton was a parliamentarian and was largely responsible for British antislavery legislation in the nineteenth century. His own professional interests, however, were not in banking—but brewing! There is more than one way to get *a–head* in business.

• • •

For further reading: James Walvin, *The Quakers: Money and Morals* (London: John Murray, 1997).

Barclays Bank headquarters in London

Lloyds Bank in the city where the firm began— Birmingham

Blessed assurance

Reading the financial pages of the newspaper would not seem to be the way to find allusions to Quakers—unless non–Quaker products such as Quaker Oats, Quaker State Motor Oil, Old Quaker Whiskey, and William Penn Cigars are mentioned! The London *Times* business section for 19 August 1998, however, carried a lead article on the deal by which Friends Provident had agreed to buy one of its main rivals in the insurance business.

"A sweet organisation that has grown from its Quaker roots into a £25 billion force to be reckoned with," as the paper described Friends Provident, the insurer was nonetheless tweaked for seemingly "aggressive and unmutual" behavior.

Such comportment, indeed, such assets, could hardly have been envisioned by the company's founders. The origins of Friends Provident go back to 1828, when a fever epidemic at the English Quaker boarding school of Ackworth resulted in the death of thirty year old teacher, Henry Brady, who left with little means of support a young widow and soon–to–be–born child.

Two Ackworth alumni, Joseph Rowntree, of the chocolate family, and Samuel Tuke, of the mental hospital family (hmm...chocolate/addiction/obsession—I see a pattern emerging) were concerned that adequate provision be made for teachers at Friends institutions. They initiated an effort to provide life assurance which resulted in the founding of the Friends Provident Institution in 1832.

Friends Provident is no longer under the control of Quakers, although the newspaper described it as "Quaker–linked." I wonder if they can assure us of that?

• • •

For further reading: Paul H. Emden, *Quakers in Commerce* (London: Sampson Low, Marston & Co., Ltd., 1939).

Ackworth School

The Retreat, pioneering Quaker mental hospital in York

The Friends Provident building in London

Envelope, please!

On London's ITV evening news of 3 November 1998, Chancellor of the Exchequer Gordon Browne's report to Parliament on the British economy was given considerable attention. Commentary on Browne's "state of the economy" included an interview with a spokesman at the accounting firm of PricewaterhouseCoopers—a company associated in the American mind more with Academy Awards tabulations than green–visored accounting wonks.

Quakers, however, ought to associate the venerable firm with Friends' storied associations with the honest pursuit of money. PricewaterhouseCoopers traces its origins to 1849, when Samuel Lowell Price set up shop in London. A member of a dissenting religious sect, he was joined in 1865 by Edwin Waterhouse, raised a Quaker.

According to historians of the company, Waterhouse was the main influence on the success of the enterprise. He cultivated his Quaker connections by landing his first major account with Friend John Fowler, a manufacturer of steam–powered agricultural equipment. His association with the Quaker Lloyds helped secure a contract with that family's prestigious bank. Among other contributions to Price Waterhouse, Edwin Waterhouse also instituted a non–smoking policy—ascribed to his "ingrained Quaker mores."

Quakers continued in prominent positions in the firm into the twentieth century, even as it grew into one of the world's largest accounting companies (in 1994 it had 450 offices in 118 countries) and helped maintain the company's reputation of "non–conformity."

Edwin Waterhouse, though, eventually was baptized into the Church of England. There's just no accounting for some people!

• • •

For further reading: David Burns Windsor, *The Quaker Enterprise: Friends in Business* (London: Frederick Muller, Ltd., 1980).

Site of Edwin Waterhouse's accounting office
at 44 Gresham Street, London

Putting your money where your house is

Among the several deadly hurricanes that lashed the Gulf Coast of the United States in the 1990s, one of the more powerful was Danny, which cut a swath of flooding and destruction through Alabama in July 1997. During the height of the storm, the front page of the *News & Record* carried a picture showing flood damage from the storm in Fairhope, Alabama. There is not much *Quakerly* about a hurricane: except for the Waterite faction, Friends avoid liquid baptism, and Quaker bluster is usually harmless! The town of Fairhope, however, can claim Quaker associations.

Fairhope was founded as a "Single Tax Colony" in 1895, with many of the families settling there arriving from the Conservative Friends communities of Iowa, Kansas, North Carolina, and Ohio. A Friends meeting was officially recognized in 1919, affiliating with Stillwater Quarterly Meeting of the Wilburite Ohio Yearly Meeting. Those familiar with the Quaker "name game" will recognize among the founders such old ethnic Friends families as Brown, Guindon, Mendenhall, and Rockwell.

These settlers were concerned for proper stewardship of the land and committed to the "single tax" economic principles formulated by Henry George, a Philadelphia Episcopalian and land reform economist. George's 1879 book, *Progress and Poverty*, popularized the theory that the idle landowner benefits from increased rents because economic progress in a locality makes land scarcer—and hence more expensive. George advocated abolishing all taxes save a tax on economic rent.

George's principles were based on the doctrine of rent and wages that economists call "Ricardian," named after the "father of political economics," London economist David Ricardo. Ricardo, himself, has his own Quaker connections. Born in 1772 of Dutch Jewish origins, in 1793 he married the Quaker Priscilla Anne Wilkinson and, though not joining Friends, was associated with them, especially in his championing of fair wage practices and his critique of the Corn Laws which made the price of grain imported into England outrageously expensive.

Other communities in the United States have been founded by Friends with similar economic interests. The "land trust" communities of Celo, North Carolina, and the Pennsylvania villages of Tanguy and Bryn Gweled have fifty–year histories and are still thriving. Fairhope, however, is unrecognizable today as a Quaker community, and that isn't just because of Hurricane Danny's fury! A small Friends meeting remains, but the original Quaker families are long removed, some having left in the 1950s to help establish the Quaker community of Monteverde in Costa Rica. The Georgist principles established

Bryn Gweled, north of Philadelphia

at Fairhope's birth are similarly nowhere to be seen, and the town looks and functions like any other Gulf Coast municipality. I won't draw any conclusions about divine retribution on the good people of Fairhope for abandoning its "trust." They probably just found it too *taxing*!

• • •

For further reading: Steven Lord, *Henry George: Dreamer or Realist?* (Philadelphia: University of Pennsylvania Press, 1965).

Building a sense of Quaker architecture

Reporter Ian Jack comments, in an article in Britain's *Independent* of 30 January 1999, on "the unknown architectural gems" in England that are old nonconformist "chapels," church buildings that are increasingly under the threat of demolition. Numbering some seventeen thousand, as many as the established Church of England counts among its parishes, these "congregationalist" places of worship are often derided as "plain preaching boxes."

Although not mentioned in the article, Friends meetinghouses would also be counted among these numerous "boxes." Friends are also "nonconformist" in Britain, and although little preaching occurs anymore in Britain's unprogrammed meetings, the buildings certainly *are* plain boxes! And they are, indeed, architectural gems.

As a dissenting sect, Quakers were prevented from building meetinghouses by the Conventicle and Quaker Acts of the 1660s. These laws forbade holding worship except in accordance with the Anglican Book of Common Prayer. Quaker places of worship—often in houses, taverns, and other "secular" places—were ransacked, stripped of furnishings, and sometimes pulled down.

In more remote or tolerant regions of the country, Friends did succeed in erecting meetinghouses before the Declaration of Indulgence in 1688 and Toleration Act of 1689 made it legal. Following Puritan lines of plainness and adopting a barn–like style to avoid detection, meetinghouses such as Adderbury (near Birmingham) and

Brigflatts (near Firbank Fell in the north), both built in 1675, still stand.

One of the meetinghouses built before Toleration was not so lucky. The Ratliff Meeting in London was pulled down, but Friends

Adderbury Friends Meeting, built 1675

continued to meet on the rubble. When troops came to disperse even this meeting for worship, Friends were cudgeled and, in at least one instance, a Friend's hat was knocked off his head and flung over the wall.

It is said that the hat sailed into a crowd that had assembled to watch the excitement, hitting one bystander who, in a Zen–like flash of enlightenment, determined to become a Quaker!

This may be the answer to the perplexing question of how to conduct Quaker evangelizing! We could recruit young Friends from the Ultimate Frisbee teams at our non–combative Quaker schools and, equipped with broad–brimmed hats, send them "into all the world, *bop*–tizing in Truth's name!"

But back to meetinghouses. Among the first legally built Friends meetinghouses in England were Jordans (briefly described in the following essay) and Colthouse, both in 1688 and both still adopting the "boxy" style. The Colthouse meetinghouse provided shelter for a congregation of Friends who had been meeting for worship in their burial ground, into whose walls they had built stone slabs as benches!

Rumor has it that people were just *dying* to get into the meeting! This may also have been the origin of the great line of Quaker Coffins!

• • •

For further reading: David M. Butler, *Quaker Meeting Houses of the Lake Counties* (London: Friends Historical Society, 1978).

Current Ratliff Friends Meeting, London

Stone benches in the Colthouse Friends burial ground

Looked over Jordans and what did I see?

During his career as a heavy–metal rocker, Ozzy Osbourne has generated his share of controversy. (Remember his taste for bats?) More recently, a bright orange glow generated by powerful floodlights erected around his suburban London estate is driving Osbourne's neighbors *batty*. According to London's *Sunday Times* of 29 November 1998, the neighbors claim that the lights—put up so Ozzy can garden at night—are ruining the night sky. The location of this dark tale? Buckinghamshire's old village of Jordans.

As the article itself mentions, Jordans is a former Quaker town, although its significance to Friends is just a footnote to the writer's main interest in shedding light on Osbourne's row with other villagers. In its Quaker heyday, the area around Jordans was home to such Quaker luminaries as William Penn and his wives Gulielma and Hannah; Christian mystics, Isaac and Mary Penington; and John Milton's secretary and editor of George Fox's *Journal,* Thomas Ellwood. All are buried in the plain graveyard adjoining the meeting-house. Revered humanitarian and political economist, John Bellers, lived in Jordans when he wrote his proposal for a "Colledge of Industry" in 1695. So did Joseph Rule, nicknamed the "white Quaker" for his undyed clothing and white house, pony, Bible, walking stick, and long beard. When Rule, too, was buried in the Jordans cemetery—next to most of these other Friends—it snowed!

The Friends meetinghouse itself is significant. Built in the late 1680s after Friends were finally allowed a measure of religious toleration, its interior is the backdrop for some of the best–loved Quaker art. J. Doyle Penrose's famous *The Presence in the Midst* and Walter West's depiction of a Quaker wedding, *The Promise*, are both set inside Jordans meetinghouse. Also nearby is the "Mayflower Barn," whose interior beams are widely reputed to have come from the Pilgrims' ship after it was broken up.

Jordans villagers have a history of steely determination. When U.S. organizers of the 1876 Centennial Exposition made attempts to rebury William Penn in Philadelphia, the meeting resisted all efforts. Legend has it that the clerk chided Pennsylvanians that they had not done such a great job living up to Penn's principles and doubted that having his moldering body would improve their record much! His remains continue to rest where he had requested.

Seems it would be advisable in the face of such resolve for Ozzy Osbourne to take a page from the Quaker book and mind the light!

• • •

For further reading: Arthur L. Hayward, *Jordans* (London: Friends Home Service Committee, 1969).

Jordans Friends Meeting, 1688–89

Getting the lay of the land

An article in a November 1996 issue of the *News & Record* reported that visitors to a poor area of Philadelphia had recently been held up by a man who pulled a gun out of a hollowed–out Bible. Sounds like the thief had misunderstood his pastor's plea to *hallow* the scripture!

It also sounds vaguely reminiscent of another Philadelphian who used a hollowed–out Bible for holier purposes. In the early 1700s, the radical antislavery Quaker activist Benjamin Lay, perturbed by the yearly meeting's slow response to various remonstrances against Friends' holding slaves, chose to make a dramatic appearance at the meetinghouse where yearly meeting was in session.

A hunchback midget who lived in a crude home dug into a hillside and who spoke with a heavy German accent, Lay already struck quite a remarkable figure, but this day he was even more unusual in appearance. Legend has undoubtedly embellished the story, but in one version of the story, Lay appeared dressed in his plain Quaker overcoat, which concealed a military uniform underneath, complete with a sword at his side.

Emotionally declaring that Friends' complicity with slavery was like "plunging a sword through the very heart of the Gospel," he threw off his coat, drew the sword, and plunged it into the Bible he was carrying, which he had earlier hollowed out to hold a pig's bladder filled with red berry juice! (Another version had him stabbing a bladder concealed in his coat.)

The "blood" splattered bystanders, and Lay was ushered out of the meeting, his pleas continuing to fall on deaf ears—evidently an early Quaker version of the repudiated Australian saloon sport of dwarf–tossing!

• • •

For further reading: John M. Moore, ed., *Friends in the Delaware Valley: Philadelphia Yearly Meeting 1681–1981* (Haverford: Friends Historical Association, 1981).

Out in left field

Quakers might be expected to excel at such a sport as baseball. After all, until recently the standard–issue uniform was *gray* flannel, and the rules of the game dictate no time limit on a game—not unlike the testimony that Friends meetings for worship are to have "no appointed ending." We'll skip over the complaint by many that baseball is too boring, even though some Friends may find *that* appealing, too.

Whatever the reason, many Quakers have distinguished themselves in the sport, as we are reminded by a feature in the *News & Record* of 29 September 1997 about the history of Guilford College baseball. The article began by noting that Pittsburgh Pirate star infielder Tony Womack, a Guilford alumnus, led the National League in 1997 with sixty stolen bases. Evidently he was asleep during discussions on campus about the Quaker testimony on integrity; that or he is counted among the "fast" Friends!

Actually, Tony is not a Friend, but such Guilford graduates as baseball legends Rick Ferrell, Tom Zachary, and Ernie Shore were Quakers from various meetings in North Carolina. Ferrell, a Hall of Fame catcher with the Detroit Tigers of the 1920s and 1930s, started behind the plate at the first All–Star Game in 1933. Zachary and Shore, both pitchers, never made it to Cooperstown's Hall of Fame, but they share peculiar honors in connection with the "Sultan of Swat," the great Babe Ruth.

Washington Senator Tom Zachary gave up Ruth's sixtieth home run in 1927—the standard of slugging until Roger Maris hit sixty–one in 1961, and Mark McGwire topped that with seventy in 1998.

Ernie Shore figures in the oddest Ruthian box score line. The Babe was a star pitcher for the Boston Red Sox in the 1910s before being traded to the New York Yankees and was once ejected from a game for arguing a called ball four on the leadoff batter. Ernie Shore came on in relief of Ruth, the batter who walked was caught attempting to steal second base, and Shore proceeded to retire the next twenty–six hitters in order. He was credited with pitching a "perfect game," since twenty–seven outs were recorded while he was pitching.

See; it *is* the ideal sport for Friends. Didn't George Fox believe in the possibility of *perfection*?

• • •

For further reading: Herb Appenzeller, *Pride in the Past* (Greensboro, NC: Guilford College Quaker Club, 1987).

Grave of Hall of Famer, Rick Ferrell, in the
New Garden (North Carolina) Friends cemetery

Whose line is it anyway?

Well–known U.S. television weatherman and huckster, Willard Scott, led off his segment of NBC's "Today Show" on 16 September 1996 with the familiar Quaker Oats Company slogan, "There's nothing better for thee than me!" Of course, the venerable oatmeal company is no more Quaker than Old Quaker Whiskey or Billy Penn Gutters, although imbibing in the one may lead to a life in the other!

In the 1980s, Quaker children and students at Friends schools nationwide successfully petitioned the Quaker Oats Company to end an advertising campaign that featured cartoon character Popeye beating up people to the refrain of, "I'm Popeye the Quaker man." "Real Quakers don't beat people up," the children argued, "nor do they treat women the way Popeye treats Olive Oyl!"

Although we can't claim Friendly origins for the oatmeal slogan (or for the company's commercial sentiments), several other familiar slogans and aphorisms do have a Quaker connection.

Many believe that "country hicks" is related to the pejorative description given by Orthodox urban Friends to the predominantly rural Hicksite Quakers of the nineteenth century. "What in the Sam Hill" refers to the eccentric Philadelphia engineer and architect, Samuel Hill, who supervised the building of the scenic Columbia River Gorge highway in Oregon, as well as erecting along the western Columbia a replica of Stonehenge and a palatial mansion for his wife. Bemused onlookers at his various building projects are reputed to have shaken their heads and clucked, "What in the world is Sam Hill up to now?"

Although popularly ascribed to Ralph Waldo Emerson, the famous phrase "I shall not pass this way again" was uttered by French–born nineteenth century evangelical Quaker minister Stephen Grellet —presumably *not* after passing one of Sam Hill's projects!

Of course, the most famous utterance by a Quaker in the twentieth century may be President Richard Nixon's "I am not a crook."

Hill's Stonehenge replica

Samuel Hill's grave along the Columbia River

42

Gussied up like a Philadelphia (no, _Indiana_) lawyer

You can take your pick of mention by the media in 1998–99 of President Bill Clinton's personal attorney, David Kendall. Thanks to Monica Lewinsky's violation of the wartime dictum, "Loose lips sink ships (of state)," Kendall was catapulted into almost daily exposure in the press—but at least not the same sort of exposure for which his boss became infamous. Such attention could hardly have been imagined for a small–town Indiana boy raised in a devout Quaker home in Western Yearly Meeting—one of our country's primarily evangelical, pastoral bodies of Friends. A law school friend of Clinton's, Kendall got to make legal history in the "trial of the century," the impeachment of the president.

Mention of Kendall in Britain's _Independent_ of 21 January 1999 stands out from the other media attention, though, as it refers to his Quaker upbringing. In an article detailing the personal histories of Clinton's defense team, the paper singles out Kendall alone to comment on his religious background. Of note in the article is a glaring violation of the journalist's law of economizing on words. Along with describing Kendall as a Quaker, the writer goes on to add that he has a "dour demeanor but dry sense of humor."

Of _course_ he is "dour and dry"! Once the fact of his Quakerism is established, that description becomes redundant!

Clinton's impeachment has its share of Quaker irony. Howard Coble, a Republican congressman from North Carolina and graduate of Quaker Guilford College, served on the House Judiciary Committee, where he voted with the majority in bringing articles of impeachment against the president.

The last time a Quaker lawyer figured so prominently in presidential impeachment intrigue was when notorious Quaker Richard Nixon (whose own grandparents were Indiana Friends) resigned his office before he could be impeached for violating at least one major Quaker testimony in the Watergate scandal: honesty!

And who might have been one of his staunchest defenders on the House Judiciary Committee at that time? David Worth Dennis, Republican congressman, Earlham College graduate, and Indiana Quaker!

• • •

For further information: Frank Mankiewicz, *U.S.* vs. *Richard Nixon: The Final Crisis* (New York: Ballantine, 1975).

Friends in high places

President Clinton's impeachment in 1999 sent pundits scampering back in history to look at the last U.S. president to be impeached. That would be Andrew Johnson, who became president upon the death of Abraham Lincoln in 1865. Johnson escaped the ignominy of being removed from office by a narrower margin than Clinton's acquittal: one scant vote. Johnson's trial before the U.S. Senate was for the alleged "high crime and misdemeanor" of forcing Edwin Stanton's removal as secretary of war.

Stanton, born into a Steubenville, Ohio, Quaker family, served as secretary of war during the Civil War under Quaker–descended Abraham Lincoln. Stanton gained respect for keeping the Union army well–equipped and fighting fit and continued in the position into Johnson's presidency. However, Johnson sought to replace him with General Ulysses S. Grant, the hero of the Union forces' victory. (Later President Grant, himself, connected with Friends when his Quaker–educated Seneca Indian adviser convinced him to invite Friends to take over major superintendencies of the Indian Bureau.)

Friends seem to have an uncanny habit of surfacing in connection with impeachment proceedings. Quaker David Worth Dennis, mentioned as one of Richard Nixon's last supporters in Congress during the Watergate scandal, finally changed his mind when "the smoking gun" of the White House tapes was revealed. Except for Edwin Stanton, most Friends *do* have an aversion to blazing weaponry!

• • •

For further reading: Fletcher Pratt, *Stanton: Lincoln's Secretary of War* (Westport, CT: Greenwood Press, 1970).

What a Payne!

In the *Times* of London on 12 January 1999, a smiling Hillary Rodham Clinton is shown holding up a book, *White House History*, with Dolley Madison's picture on its cover. It is hard to figure the significance of the photo—it accompanies an article titled "Clinton trial set for operatic climax." Neither Hillary nor Dolley appears to be singing, let alone anywhere near "climax." It is easier, however, to connect the picture with Friends.

A first connection is with the city of Washington, D.C. itself. Our country's first planned city, Washington was designed by the eccentric French urban planner Charles–Pierre L'Enfant, but a Quaker, James Thornton, carried out much of the actual work.

Dolley Madison herself was born into a New Garden, North Carolina, Quaker family in 1768. Dolley was very young when the family moved to Virginia, where her parents became clerks of their new Friends meeting. After freeing their slaves and having to sell their plantation, the Payne family moved again when Dolley was fifteen, this time to Philadelphia.

In the Quaker City, Dolley married John Todd, but she was left a young widow when Todd and their newborn baby died of yellow fever in 1793. She did not remain unmarried for long, though. James Madison met her later that year, and they were married in 1794.

Even after marrying the non–Quaker Madison, Dolley continued to use the plain speech and to dress in her Quaker clothes at home. This pattern continued in the White House when Madison became president, although she confessed that, when the British were burning

Washington in 1814, she, while remaining a Quaker in her mind, advocated fighting when assaulted!

It was from the commencement terrace of Washington's Sidwell Friends School, ringed by a hedge of boxwoods grown from a sprig of Dolley Madison's inauguration bouquet, that President Bill Clinton addressed his daughter Chelsea's graduating class in 1997. During that address, Clinton commented on how much he had enjoyed Sidwell's Quaker meeting for worship. He described how people gathered in the silence and spoke only when "they had something meaningful to say." He went on to add, "I wish Congress were under the control of the Quakers!"

I don't think so! Friends used to disown folks for doing what he did in the Oval Office.

• • •

For further reading: Ella Kent Barnard, *Dorothy Payne, Quakeress* (Philadelphia: Ferris & Leach, 1909).

Dolley Madison
Courtesy of the Greensboro Historical Museum

Roll out the Quaker Cannons

Many press reports about Newt Gingrich's stepping down as Speaker of the House of Representatives after the Republican Party's poor showing in the November 1998 elections recalled the happier days (and Quaker allusions) when he first became Speaker after the 1994 elections. At that time some papers compared him to one of the last influential Republican Speakers of the House: Joseph "Uncle Joe" Gurney Cannon, after whom the congressional Cannon Office Building is named.

As Quakerphiles would readily recognize from Cannon's full name, he had Quaker roots. Born in the New Garden, North Carolina, Quaker community in 1836, he moved with his family to the Midwest, where he became a student in the Friends Boarding School in Richmond, Indiana. He went on to be elected to Congress from Illinois, serving for a total of forty–six years and becoming a powerful Speaker, occupying that position 1903–11. His importance was such that his face graced the cover of the very first issue of *Time* magazine.

This little piece of Quaker history whets the appetite for more Friends in politics—of whom there have been too many to mention all (and some we would rather *not* mention). In this space we will stick only to the U.S. presidents. The obvious ones are Herbert Hoover (an Iowa Quaker) and Richard Nixon (whose ancestors were the model for the fictionalized Birdwell Quaker family in the Hollywood film *Friendly Persuasion.*) There are more, however.

According to the book *Albion's Seed,* Abraham Lincoln had Quaker ancestors on both sides, and his mother, Nancy Hanks, was a

North Carolina Quaker. William McKinley and Grover Cleveland had Quaker grandmothers; Warren G. Harding's mother was a Quaker, and, to be politic, we must mention that the Confederacy's one president, Jefferson Davis, was descended from Welsh Quakers who had settled in Pennsylvania. And I'm not just "whistling Dixie" (which, by the way, gets its name from the Mason–Dixon Line, one of whose surveyors, Jeremiah Dixon, was an English Quaker instrument maker)!

• • •

For further reading: L. White Busbey, *Uncle Joe Cannon* (New York: H. Holt & Co., 1927).

*Plaque honoring Joseph Gurney Cannon
on the campus of Guilford College*

The witness of
Norman Morrison

A front page photo in the *Times* of London on 17 February 1999 shows a fifteen year old Kurdish girl who had set herself ablaze at London's Greek Embassy to protest a perceived Greek betrayal of a Kurdish rebel leader. On the next page, under the headline "Martyrs who fanned the flames of protest," Robin Young gives a brief history of self–immolation as a means of political protest.

According to his article, "the most famous self–immolator is Jan Palach," a twenty–one year old Czech student who set himself ablaze in Prague's Wenceslas Square in 1969 to protest his government's complicity with Soviet occupation. He, in turn, was probably influenced by the 1963 self–immolation in Saigon of Buddhist monk Thich Quang Duc, as a witness against the Diem regime's repressive policies. The picture of his body burning in lotus position became a famous icon of protest during the American war in Vietnam.

Unmentioned in the article is the self–sacrifice of American Quaker Norman Morrison in 1965, an action that profoundly shook Washington's corridors of power and led to much soul–searching among Friends.

On 2 November 1965, Morrison, having a cold, stayed home from his work as Baltimore Monthly Meeting (Stony Run) executive secretary. He made no remarkable comments to his wife, Anne, before she left that afternoon to pick up a son and daughter from school. Norman remained behind with their one–year old, Emily.

While Anne was away, Norman drove with Emily into nearby Washington, and, in the early evening as thousands of workers were streaming out of the Pentagon, he doused himself with gasoline, cradled his daughter in his arms, and set himself on fire in front of the building's main entrance.

Before the flames reached his daughter, he set Emily down and calmly burned to death.

Norman Morrison was born in 1933 into a devout Pennsylvania Presbyterian family. He received his advanced education at a Presbyterian college and seminary in the United States before going with his new wife, Anne, to Scotland for further theological study at the University of Edinburgh. While there, they attended the local Friends meeting, continuing an association with Friends begun in the States, and in 1959 they joined Friends at the Pittsburgh Meeting.

Almost immediately the Morrisons engaged themselves in vital Quaker work; they served as directors of the Charlotte, North Carolina, Friends Center for two years, during which time Norman was deeply involved in the South's civil rights struggle. In 1962 they moved to Baltimore, where Norman began service as Stony Run's executive secretary.

His involvement in civil rights and peace concerns intensified, and he grew more and more deeply troubled by the world's seemingly inexorable march to the brink of nuclear holocaust. Images of the maiming, burning, and killing of innocents in the American war against the people of Vietnam increasingly troubled him.

In the 1 December 1965 *Friends Journal*, his widow concluded her obituary for Norman with these words:

> Norman Morrison was convinced that the control and ultimate elimination of war is an imperative of this century. He considered war itself—and the hatred and passions it inspires—the real enemy of the peoples of Vietnam and the United States. On November 2, 1965 he gave his life as witness to this belief.

In his memoir, Robert McNamara, in 1965 the United States secretary of defense pursuing his government's Vietnam war policy, states how deeply affected he was by Morrison's sacrifice, an event which occurred only forty feet from his office in the Pentagon.

McNamara admits that Morrison's death was an outcry against the killing that was destroying so many lives.

North Vietnam responded by issuing a postage stamp with Morrison's likeness and (misspelled) name against a background of flames; and "Emily, My Child," a Vietnamese poem about the Morrison's daughter, was memorized by students.

Four days before his death, Norman Morrison delivered a manuscript of a meditation to the *Friends Journal* office in Philadelphia, with no hint that it would serve, along with his wife's eulogy, as a memorial. In part, it read:

> In communion with our Creator all the music that is playing upon the theme of self–interest falls silent. There is a completeness which allows life to be like a new drop of freshly fallen rain, a self–fulfilling junction of the finite and the infinite. Our enemies remain within as well as without, and satisfaction is but one more temporary illusion. Once we accept this premise, it is clear that life will be a strenuous contest. No religion could long endure a hero whose goal was the personal satisfaction of his cause.

Indeed, it could be said that Norman Morrison was not satisfied in his cause. He was consumed by it.

• • •

For further reading: Robert S. McNamara, *In Retrospect: The Tragedy and Lessons of Vietnam* (New York: Times Books, 1995).

The Darbys of Coalbrookdale

Quakers have been described as having iron wills, and any who have attended a Quaker potluck/carry–in/covered dish/pitch–in/bring–and–share meal knows that one requirement for being a Friend is a cast–iron stomach. A BBC radio public service announcement helps us realize that this association of Quakers with metal goes way back.

During February and March 1999, as part of Britains's "Step into History" campaign on the BBC radio network, a series of messages featured a child's voice excitedly reciting all the wonders Abraham Darby I, II, and III had created at their foundries in the Severn River Valley. We would have been more excited if she had mentioned that they all were Quakers.

Abraham Darby I (1677–1717) was raised in a Quaker family, was apprenticed to a Quaker ironworker and malter, and made one of the most crucial contributions to the Industrial Revolution when he perfected the use of coke in smelting iron, a process he first observed as a young apprentice. Not only did he improve the quality and increase the quantity of iron produced by this method, he freed charcoal for much more important purposes: backyard barbecues!

Abraham Darby II (1711–1763) continued the legacy at the family's Coalbrookdale foundries and saw the introduction of steam power and the casting of steam engine parts and frames for screw-presses added to the company's innovations, each fueling the engine of England's burgeoning industry. He also gradually eliminated a product line other family members had introduced before he was old enough to take over the reins of business from his father: cannons!

Abraham Darby III (1750–1789) expanded the foundries and plant of the Coalbrookdale company, built schools, provided improved housing for his workers, and built the world's first iron bridge in 1779, a structure that still spans the Severn River in the town that has come to be known as Ironbridge.

For all these significant contributions to the Industrial Age, the Severn Valley has been named a World Heritage Site—along with Stonehenge, the Pyramids, and other wonders. The Coalbrookdale Company name is preserved on the iron gates still standing on the site in London's Hyde Park where they opened the world to the 1851 Great Exposition and the grandeur of Victorian England's Crystal Palace.

But the Darbys—and others—paid a price for their success. Darbys I and III died at the young age of thirty–nine, and many workers in primitive foundry conditions—often likened to hell—suffered similarly shortened lives. The region was blighted for years from the smoke, waste, mining slag, and exhaustion of resources that the iron industry inflicted.

Although the natural beauty of the valley has made a remarkable comeback, such connection of Friends with the negative side of the Industrial Revolution certainly tests our *mettle*!

• • •

For further reading: Arthur Raistrick, *Dynasty of Iron Founders* (York: Sessions Book Trust, 1989).

The iron bridge, 1779

Friends in training

Less than humble and modest Friends have been known to "railroad" pet concerns through committees; other Friends have been accused of possessing a "one–track" mind when it comes to peace, equality, simplicity, or another such pet testimony. A few have been described as being "one or two carriages short of a full train." An article on 12 December 1998 in the *Times* of London reminds us that Quakers and railroading, in fact, go way back!

The first new steam locomotive to be built in Britain in forty years was the occasion for the article, which noted the hope of workers at the Darlington Locomotive Works that the engine would be completed by 27 September 2000. That date would coincide with the 175th anniversary of the opening of the Stockton & Darlington Railway, the world's first public railway.

The Quaker Edward Pease had proposed a railway between these two English towns for more efficient shipment of freight. In 1821 he received a royal assent to build a line that would utilize the new technologies of iron making and steam power on a grander scale.

A noted engineer, George Stephenson, convinced Pease of the potential of steam locomotives for the enterprise, having successfully developed a stationary steam engine earlier. When the rail line opened in 1825, one of Stephenson's engines pulled the first load. Eight years later, a steam engine was first used to pull a passenger train on the Stockton & Darlington.

Developments by English Quaker ironmasters in the eighteenth century paved the way for the age of steam railroading. The Darbys had pioneered in laying down cast iron rails at their Coalbrookdale forges to haul wagons of coke and pig iron and had invented the flanged wheel to keep the wagons on the rails.

No wonder one of Quakerdom's favorite hymns is "Blest Be the Tie That Binds."

• • •

For further reading: Maurice W. Kirby, *The Origins of Railway Enterprise: the Stockton & Darlington Railway, 1821–1863* (Cambridge University Press, 1993).

Old Cadbury chocolate works steam engine,
now at work on the Welsh railway in Llangollen

I've looked at clouds
from both sides now

To celebrate the 250th birthday of Johan Wolfgang von Goethe, England's Corydon Singers and Orchestra, specialists in German Romantic music, presented a concert of vocal and instrumental music inspired by the great German's writings. A review of the concert in the *Times* of London on 26 January 1999 noted both the excellence of the musical interpretations of Goethe's poems *and* the fine pun in the concert's title: "Goethe Nacht."

Nothing obviously Quaker about this, unless one counts any pun as evocative of Friends' preferred form of humor. But here we are not above celebrating the influence on Goethe of a little–known Quaker, Luke Howard.

Howard, who died in 1864 at the age of ninety–two, is best known among meteorologists, who still use the classification of clouds he invented in 1803: cirrus, cumulus, stratus, nimbus, etc. Meteorology and botany were the English Friend's hobbies; professionally he was an apothecary, working for a time in partnership with the famous Quaker chemist and humanitarian, William Allen, and maintaining a close relationship with John Dalton, the Quaker scientist who developed the atomic theory of chemistry.

Howard's writings on cloud formations captured the attention of Goethe, himself an amateur meteorologist, and he wrote a poem about clouds dedicated to him—*Howards Ehrengedächtnis* (In Honor of Howard). In 1822 Goethe wrote Howard asking that he send him an autobiographical essay. Goethe was delighted with Howard's self-description, the Quaker's "practical mysticism," and his sincere and devout religious belief. Howard was thereafter referred to by Goethe as "our master."

In addition to interests in science and impressing German Romanticists, Howard kept up an active philanthropic life. He participated in relief work to German lands devastated by Napoleon's armies, campaigned against slavery, and was an active member of the British and Foreign Bible Society.

Howard left Quakers and joined the Plymouth Brethren in the wake of the 1835 Beaconite theological storm that broke over British Quakerism. Given his great contributions to society in science and service, however, we'll not call him a "fair weather Friend."

• • •

For further reading: D. F. S. Scott, *Luke Howard* (York: William Sessions, Ltd., 1976).

Atomic–powered Friend

In a spot on NBC's "Tonight Show" of 12 May 1999, host Jay Leno presented significant events in history and then added a comic element with a fictitious "day after" occurrence. For a day in 1803, he stated that John Dalton revealed the basis of atomic theory. The next day, Leno chortled, "The Chinese stole it!"

One may wonder what this writer was doing staying up way past "Quaker midnight" to catch a show that begins at 11:35 P.M. A more significant question may be why I was watching Leno instead of David Letterman, who is a fellow Hoosier and former hallmate of mine at Ball State University. But I digress.

Obviously I was meant to catch Leno's sketch so that I could add yet another name to the long list of Quaker scientists. God moves in mysterious ways. John Dalton (1766–1844) was a British chemist and physicist who developed the atomic theory of matter and is regarded as one of the fathers of modern physical science. He also was a Friend who held throughout his life to the faith, dress, and manners of Quakers.

Dalton was born into a family of Quaker weavers in the cradle of the movement's beginnings—Cumberland, in northwestern England. Already at the age of twelve he took charge of a Friends school, teaching for some fourteen years until he went on to be a tutor of mathematics and natural philosophy at New College in Manchester.

Like fellow Friend, Luke Howard, he developed an interest in meteorology, making important contributions to the study of the weather in his native Lake District. He also maintained an extensive collection of botanical and insect species, as well as journals of his natural observations and experiments.

As Jay Leno mentioned, in 1803 Dalton devised a system of chemical symbols and weights of atoms, arranging them into a table. He published his findings in 1808, assuring his place in the history of science. He was named a fellow of the Royal Society and received that organization's highest prize in 1825.

Consistent with his Quaker faith, Dalton was skeptical of untested authority, especially when, early in his scientific career, he found himself misled by supposed experts. He resolved to try others' opinions and findings by his own experience. One time, however, his failure to observe an important phenomenon and avoid an embarrassing mistake led to another of his major contributions to natural science.

Unaware of his own inability to distinguish colors, Dalton once bought his very proper Quaker mother a pair of red stockings! The discovery of his condition prompted him to undertake an extensive study of the causes and treatment of that problem. His contributions to this field of study were so significant that for a long time "Daltonism" was a common term for color blindness.

Perhaps this is why so many Quakers "see red" over various social issues! But at least in the case of atomic weaponry and atomic power, we can't blame John Dalton. He is responsible only for developing the theory of how matter is made up. Even as an amateur meteorologist, he couldn't have predicted what some would later do to harness the power of the atom.

And he certainly couldn't have "colored" the discussion with his Quaker sensitivities!

• • •

For further reading: Elizabeth Chambers Patterson, *John Dalton and the Atomic Theory; the biography of a natural philosopher* (New York: Doubleday, 1970).

Having a mean time
at Greenwich

An announcement that the Royal Greenwich Observatory had been permanently closed (London *Times*, 31 October 1998) alerts the Quaker observer to Friendly connections with Britain's oldest scientific institution. Established by Charles II in 1675, the Royal Greenwich Observatory's first clocks were crafted by London Friend Thomas Tompion, and the observatory was the first employer of eminent Quaker physicist, Arthur Eddington.

Tompion, "the father of English watchmaking," had achieved such a high reputation for the precision of his instruments, that he was asked while in his thirties—only three years after starting out in business for himself—to make the clocks on whose accuracy the observatory's calculations depended. Clocks by Tompion are to be found yet today in the Hampton Court, Windsor, and Buckingham palaces, as well as in the British Museum.

Arthur Eddington, knighted by the Crown for his contributions to science, was one of the few physicists who understood Einstein's theory of relativity and interpreted it for the British scientific community. Fresh out of Cambridge University in 1906, he was hired to work at the Royal Observatory. A conscientious objector during World War I, Eddington escaped the calumny visited on many other pacifists, because colleagues, recognizing his brilliance, convinced officials that he was a valuable national resource.

In 1919, Eddington confirmed Einstein's theory of relativity by observations of that year's solar eclipse. Once again, we see Friends witnessing to the Light!

• • •

For further reading: Arthur Raistrick, *Quakers in Science and Industry* (London: The Bannisdale Press, 1950).

Doctoring up Quakerism

An article in the *Times* of London on 23 October 1998 mentioned a medical term that was to be heard frequently during the final illness of Jordan's King Hussein, and every time his condition was described, a great Quaker medical doctor, Thomas Hodgkin, was brought to mind, even if few today know much about the plain British Friend.

The article reported that King Hussein suffered from "non–Hodgkin's lymphoma," a type of cancer that primarily affects the lymph nodes and spleen. Hodgkin's Disease, a rare disease resembling both inflammation and cancer, usually of the lymph nodes, takes its name from the Quaker physician who first described it in 1832. Although others went on to analyze the disease more thoroughly, an admirer of Hodgkin's work, Dr. Samuel Wilks, attached Hodgkin's name to the disease.

Hodgkin had pioneered in the use of the stethoscope and was an early advocate of the microscope, even though his observations on the lymphatic system had actually been done without the instrument. But his brilliance as a scientist and as a doctor at Guy's Hospital in London did not save his medical career from being effectively scuttled by his adherence to Quaker principle. When he applied for an important post at Guy's in 1837, his candidacy was opposed by the hospital's head, Benjamin Harrison (and not the one who died of pneumonia after being inaugurated president of the United States on a brutally cold day).

Harrison, who served on the board of the fur–trading Hudson's Bay Company, had been offended by Hodgkin's criticism of the company's treatment of Canadian Native Americans. Failing to receive the position, Hodgkin left the practice of medicine and spent the rest of his life working for such causes as antislavery and aboriginal rights. He died in 1866 in Jaffa, Palestine, while accompanying the Jewish philanthropist Moses Montefiore on a humanitarian mission. He died of a Hodgkin–related illness, but it wasn't lymphoma!

Actually, it was cholera, and Hodgkin was buried in a graveyard on the grounds of the Church of Scotland's Tabitha Girls School in Jaffa. Montefiore had a rather un–Quakerly marker erected on his friend's grave, one of two markers financed by him in the region. The other is Rachel's Tomb, the mausoleum near Bethlehem at the reputed site of the biblical matriarch's burial.

• • •

For further reading: Michael Rose, *Curator of the Dead: Thomas Hodgin* (London: Peter Owen, 1981).

Grave of Thomas Hodgkin in Jaffa, Israel

Friends with X–ray vision

Quakers and crystals! It conjures up images of New Age Friends building pyramid–shaped meetinghouses to sharpen their meditation skills, or wearing quartz pendants to refract their Inward Light. But, no, this association is brought to mind by a book review in the *Times* of London on 21 January 1999.

Georgiana Ferry's biography of X–ray crystallographer Dorothy Hodgkin made no mention of yet another Hodgkin Quaker scientist, probably because Dorothy (*née* Crowfoot) Hodgkin was not a Friend! She had a string of important Quaker associations, however, not the least of which was with her husband, Thomas Hodgkin. He had been a history lecturer with the Friends Voluntary Service, working with unemployed miners in the 1930s, and was a distant relative of the Thomas Hodgkin of Hodgkin's Disease fame. Dorothy and Thomas met in the home of a Hodgkin relative and Quaker, Margery Fry, principal of Somerville College, Oxford, and niece of Joseph Storrs Fry, the Quaker chocolate magnate.

Dorothy was a younger contemporary and acquaintance of Quaker crystallographer Kathleen Lonsdale, whose biography she wrote for the Royal Society shortly after Lonsdale's death in 1971. Both Lonsdale and Hodgkin had remarkably parallel careers. Lonsdale was one of the first two women elected into Britain's Royal Society for her pioneering work with X–rays in studying crystals. Hodgkin was the first English woman to win a Nobel Prize (in 1964) for solving the structures of penicillin and vitamin B–12.

Lonsdale joined Friends in 1935 out of disillusionment with the aftermath of World War I, was a conscientious objector in World War II, and became an effective champion of penal reform after her own imprisonment for refusing conscription into the fire brigades she had formerly volunteered for! Hodgkin married into Friends in 1937 and was famous for her peace activities which included trips to China and Vietnam in her later life.

The book review never mentioned the "Q" word, but with a name like Hodgkin and the article's allusions to the author's concern for gender equality and peace, Dorothy's Friendly connections should have been crystal clear!

• • •

For further reading: Dorothy Hodgkin, *Kathleen Lonsdale* (London: The Royal Society, 1976).

Yet another Hodgkin

Britain's *Independent* of 4 January 1999 gave a full–page obituary for Alan Hodgkin (1914–1998), an honor befitting a fellow of the Royal Society and a knight of the British Empire!

Within the first few paragraphs, the article mentions Hodgkin's strict Quaker upbringing. His father, George Hodgkin, was a conscientious objector during World War I and died of dysentery in Baghdad while on his way to a second tour of relief work in Armenia.

Alan became a noted experimental biologist in the areas of nerve fibre study and the mechanics of vision. He was a joint recipient of the 1963 Nobel Prize in medicine. They must have been running bargain specials on Hodgkin Nobel Prize winners in the 1960s!

Unlike his father, who refused to participate in any endeavor connected with the war effort, Alan made a significant contribution to the development of airborne radar during World War II—an innovation that contributed to the Royal Air Force's critical success in the Battle of Britain against Germany's Luftwaffe. Nonetheless, Hodgkin did oppose Churchill's policy of bombing open cities and returned to medical efforts after the war.

His Quaker convictions also were apparent in his wholehearted support of admitting women to Trinity College at Cambridge when he was named master of Trinity in 1978 and in the modesty that his colleagues recalled in this man of immodest achievement.

• • •

For further reading: Alan L. Hodgkin, *The Conduction of the Nervous Impulse* (Liverpool University Press, 1971).

No wonder Quakers are into "imaging"

Hardly a day goes by without mention in a paper somewhere in the world, or in the electronic media, of a medical procedure known as an MRI. Now, that alone would be sufficient to inspire a Quaker meditation, for—although it has yet to be confirmed by linguists—I am convinced that Friends invented acronyms! EFI, FGC, FUM, AFSC, FCNL, QUNO, FWCC, QPS, BYM, QLSP, AFCIA, FCUN, FAHE—it is enough to give one a headache or an increasingly knee–jerk objection to such Quaker "in" language!*

Which brings us to the real connection with the MRI. The Greens-boro *News & Record* of 10 September 1996 noted that the Carolina Panthers football team's quarterback, Kerry Collins, had been hit and suffered a knee injury in the most recent game. An MRI, however,

---

* The meaning of these acronyms are as follows: EFI = Evangelical Friends International; FGC = Friends General Conference; FUM = Friends United Meeting; AFSC = American Friends Service Committee; FCNL = Friends Committee on National Legislation; QUNO = Quaker United Nations Office; FWCC = Friends World Committee on Consultation; QPS = Quaker Peace and Service; BYM = Britain Yearly Meeting; QLSP = Quaker Leadership Scholars Program at Guilford College; AFCIA = American Friends Committee on Indian Affairs; FCUN = Friends Committee on Unity with Nature; and FAHE = Friends Association for Higher Education.

showed that he had sustained only a slight sprain. Collins himself is not the connection here, although he *did* attend Penn State University. Rather, the person who invented the MRI (Magnetic Resonance Imaging) is a Friend.

Waldo Hinshaw, son of Seth and Mary Edith Hinshaw, the patriarch and matriarch of latter twentieth century Carolina Quakerism, developed the now–essential medical tool while employed with Johnson & Johnson in Boston. A physics major at the University of North Carolina, Hinshaw could not find a teaching position after graduation and continued his studies at Britain's Nottingham University. While there, he attended a physics seminar in Bombay, India, where he got the idea of using magnetic resonance for medical procedures.

Too bad we didn't have the MRI in the early days of Quakerism. It would be interesting to know what really was going on inside those crazy first Friends! But then, their personal magnetism would probably have skewed the results anyway!

• • •

For further reading: James Mattson, *The Pioneers of NMR and Magnetic Resonance in Medicine: The Story of MRI* (New York: Dean Book Co., 1996).

A stellar Quaker

Readers of these essays may have noted by now that there seems to be a disproportionately large number of scientists—and especially physicists—among Friends. Perhaps it comes from George Fox's early inclination, as he records in his *Journal,* to "practice physick." Fortunately for the world, though, he went into the far more lucrative arena of public Christian ministry.

A cover article in the 20 July 1998 issue of *Newsweek* magazine about science and religion enables us to add another name to the list of notable Quakers in science. Featured in a sidebar about a select group of physicists with faith is S. Jocelyn Bell Burnell. Identified as an "astronomer and Quaker" in the article, it is said of her that "She wills herself to accept Christian theology . . . because the absence of belief is too lonely and frightening a prospect."

Burnell's credentials in the world of physics were cemented in the 1960s as a graduate student at Cambridge University. Then known as Susan Jocelyn Bell, she was working under the supervision of Antony Hewish when she observed curious regular pulses of radio signals from certain points in the sky. These pulsating radio stars, or pulsars as they became known, were the subject of the 1974 Nobel Prize in physics awarded to Cambridge radio astronomers Hewish and Martin Ryle. Bell Burnell's contribution was not acknowledged in the Nobel ceremonies, however.

When another Quaker astrophysicist, Joseph Taylor, was named a co–recipient of the 1993 Nobel Prize for his work on pulsars in binary systems and their use in testing Einstein's theory of general relativity, he remedied this oversight. He invited Jocelyn Burnell to the ceremonies as an honored guest—probably the most Quakers to appear at the awards dinner since the Religious Society of Friends itself was awarded the Nobel Peace Prize in 1947.

Burnell also has "star" quality as a Quaker. She served during the 1990s as presiding clerk of Britain Yearly Meeting, where her training as a physicist probably came in handy: it takes special knowledge to move immovable objects—especially when one knows that a fundamental law of physics is that objects at rest tend to stay at rest!

• • •

For further reading: S. Jocelyn Bell Burnell, *Broken for Life*, the 1989 Swarthmore Lecture (London: Quaker Home Service, 1989).

Sweet Friends

It is almost impossible to go anywhere in the United Kingdom without seeing the name Cadbury, in script, advertising the wares of the most famous of the Quaker–founded chocolate empires. Quakers were almost synonymous with British chocolate from the nineteenth century into the twentieth. The top three confectionery firms during that time were all owned by Friends: Fry of Bristol; Cadbury of Birmingham/Bournville; and Rowntree of York. Cadbury eventually bought out J. S. Fry and Sons, and Rowntree was taken over by Swiss foods giant Nestlé, but the Rowntree and Fry names even now survive as particular product lines within the parent companies.

An article in the *Times* of London on 17 October 1998 reminds us that the old Quaker firms were not just about amassing great fortunes courtesy of a culture's sweet tooth. The article reports on the plans of the Bournville Village Trust to build a 750–house development on 230 acres of farm land outside Birmingham.

George Cadbury had the original Bournville Village built adjacent to his new factory in 1895, to provide affordable, healthful housing in a natural, green environment—not only for workers in his plant but also for others wanting an escape from the squalor of industrial cities in England. The project was an overwhelming success and has since expanded to comprise more than one thousand acres of land with some 7,900 homes. It inspired, in turn, the Garden City Movement and served as a model for Joseph Rowntree's similar project of New Earswick near his chocolate works in York.

Quakers became involved in chocolate, in part, as a result of their

Guilford College students at the Cadbury factory in Birmingham, 1998

"teetotal" views in the nineteenth century, and, indeed, Cadbury initially allowed no alcohol in Bournville Village. To this day, the trust stipulates that no alcohol be sold in the village. Old George even cautioned against imbibing "fizzy drinks."

I wonder what he would make, then, of the fact that Cadbury is now in partnership with drinks conglomerate Schweppes and that a report in the *Times* of 12 December 1998 notes that Cadbury Schweppes distributes Dr. Pepper in the United States? Perhaps, he might echo the popular American greeting card produced by Quaker artist Sandy Boynton: "Things getting worse! Send chocolate!"

• • •

For further reading: Gillian Wagner, *The Chocolate Conscience* (Chatto & Windus, 1987) and Ian Campbell Bradley, *Enlightened Entrepreneurs* (London: Weidenfeld and Nicolson, 1987).

Woodbrooke Quaker Study Centre, former Cadbury estate in Bournville

Feeling the Quaker blues

The Religious Society of Friends may not be a household name these days, but many products developed by Friends are. Some have already been considered in these essays. Add to the list the likes of Hires Root Beer and Carnation Condensed Milk, and we begin to think that Friends do, in fact, have more "liquid assets" than we might have thought! There are other products that borrow on Quakers' good name. The obvious ones have already been mentioned, but there is also Listerine, named after Quaker–born pioneer of antiseptic surgery, Joseph Lister. That mouthwash is often used to mask the smell of William Penn Cigars on a smoker's breath.

We won't even go into consideration of intriguingly named companies such as Philadelphia's Quaker Moving and Storage (someone is always putting us in our place) or Quaker Exterminators (I thought that ended with the Act of Toleration).

A brief notice in the *Times* of London on 3 February 1999 recalls a Quaker household name of Britain's past. The article, about the chief executive of Reckitt & Colman receiving a "golden parachute" payoff of £900,000 for leaving his position, makes no mention of the company's Quaker roots. Nor would one suspect it with compensation of that magnitude! Quakers have gotten over their opposition to a "hireling" ministry but not to the extent of compensation like that.

Reckitt & Colman, Ltd. is the result of a 1938 merger between famous mustard maker, Colman, and the Quaker producer of starch and laundry bluing, Reckitt. Certainly a logical merger: ever try to get one of those yellow mustard stains out?

The Reckitt & Sons Company began in 1840 in Hull, England, when Isaac Reckitt took over a struggling starch factory. His son, James, developed the business into a large and successful one, expanding into a line of laundry products, packaged in a trademark dark blue, that dominated the market.

Typical of Quaker entrepreneurs in the Victorian era, James Reckitt carried his religious convictions into his corporate life, building a Garden Village for his employees, establishing a health plan, and introducing pension and profit–sharing schemes. He created a charitable trust that supported medical concerns, orphanages, temperance, and a variety of Quaker concerns. It also provided assistance to the Salvation Army and other urban and foreign mission endeavors.

The latter would certainly seem consistent with Reckitt & Sons interests. In those nicely starched uniforms, Salvation Army members are well–known for belting out music about being washed "whiter than snow."

Nice to be so ecumenical about it! After all, Quakers do tend to prefer *dry cleaning* to immersion in water.

• • •

For further reading: Desmond Chapman–Huston, *Sir James Reckitt, a Memoir* (London: Faber & Gwyer, 1927).

Pinning things on Quakers

It would almost seem that there was an expectation by early Friends that they be inventive, given the many creations, developments, and discoveries made by Quakers over the years. They could certainly be creative in their response to spiritual matters: just consider Fox wandering through the streets of Litchfield, barefoot in the snow, crying "Woe to you bloody city," or James Nayler riding into the city of Bristol as some of his followers waved branches and cried "Hosanna!" The creative energy that went into product development has been somewhat less controversial, although what is *done* with those products sometimes can be. With that, on to the next connection:

The *Times* of London on 6 February 1999 carried a notice about a jewelry exhibition opening at the Craze Gallery in London. The gallery would feature the work of Marie–Lise Goëlo, whose designs of rings, bracelets, necklaces, and even bustiers are all made from the humble safety pin.

Not that the humble American Quaker inventor of the safety pin, Walter Hunt, would have approved of using his creation for such un–Quakerly things—especially not bustiers, even if (as she claims) world–famous bustier wearer, singer, and actress, Madonna, does have a Quaker step–grandmother!

I am sure Hunt had no other intent for his invention than an application of the Quaker testimony on non–violence.

The location of the Craze Gallery in London's Clerkenwell section enables us to make yet another Quaker connection. In 1702, London Friends opened a workhouse for the poor in Clerkenwell.

Inspired by Quaker John Bellers' 1695 book *Proposals for a Colledge of Industry*, it did not live up to the standards of Bellers' carefully articulated response to urban poverty and illiteracy—but the workhouse also didn't make safety pin intimate apparel, either! The Clerkenwell project eventually evolved into the highly regarded Quaker boarding school, Saffron–Walden, now located outside of London.

Saffron–Walden Friends School,
descendant of Bellers' "Colledge of Industry"

But, in closing, let us go back to Quaker product development. Along with metal fabrication and comestibles, we can add the invention of the bottle cap by Baltimore Quaker Robert Painter. To railroading, we can add the Atlantic City version of the board game Monopoly, complete with the Reading and Pennsylvania lines that hint at Quaker influence; the popular game was developed by staff of the Atlantic City, New Jersey, Friends School. And to "instrument making" and transportation we can add the Flexible Flyer sled and the Slinky, both produced by companies whose inventor–founders (Samuel Allen and Robert James, respectively) were Quaker graduates of Westtown School.

As humbly proud as we might be, however, of these Quaker contributions, one might wonder at the wisdom of the last two products mentioned. Ever since their development in the first half of the twentieth century, it can be noted that Friends have been going downhill!

Maybe we've *pinned* our hopes too much on the accomplishments of previous generations of Quakers.

• • •

For further reading: A. Ruth Fry, *John Bellers* (London: Cassell & Co., Ltd., 1935).

All the Quakers one
might want—for a song

A congruence of brief snippets in the British media related to U.S. singers inspires this entry. During a BBC Radio 2 musical quiz in January 1999, listeners were asked to identify a song that turned out to be Bonnie Raitt's blues/pop hit tune "Nick of Time." The same day that quiz was running on the radio, a promotion for a program called "Girls with Guitars" featured pop singer Sarah McLachlan telling how, as a child, she loved listening to Joan Baez. Later in the same week when these singers were mentioned on Radio 2, the "Vision" magazine of the *Times* carried a picture of Emmylou Harris as advertisement for a cable TV musical concert.

What went for some unknown reason without comment by these sources can be revealed here: all three singers—Raitt, Baez, and Harris—have Quaker connections. Bonnie Raitt, daughter of Broadway star and New York Yearly Meeting Friend John Raitt, interned with the American Friends Service Committee in the 1960s. Joan Baez, too, has been associated with Friends since her attendance at Quaker meeting in Buffalo, New York, before becoming a folk–singing icon. Country star Emmylou Harris gives new meaning to the term "country hicks" as an attender at Nashville's Friends General Conference (*Hick*site)–related unprogrammed meeting.

For a religious group better known for forbidding music than for making it, Friends have produced their fair share of popular musicians. Donald Swann, a British Friend, took the West End and Broadway by storm in the 1960s with his collaborative review, *At the Drop of a Hat*. David Byrne, former lead singer for "Talking Heads," is related to a Baltimore Quaker family. Rich Mullins, the late contemporary Christian musical artist and Friends University graduate, hailed from an Indiana Quaker family. Fellow Hoosier, folk and pop singer, Carrie Newcomer, attends Bloomington Friends. Two other Quakers similarly at opposite ends of the musical spectrum come from the same Charlottesville (Virginia) meeting: folk singer, John McCutcheon, and alternative rocker, Dave Matthews.

All but Mullins from this list of Quakers are from the "silent" tradition of Friends. What did Freud say about sublimation?

We cannot close this meditation on Quaker singers without giving attention to the claim of a North Carolina evangelist, Alex McFarland, that the "Beach Boys" were influenced by Friends. A devoted Beach Boys fan, he notes that some of the group's members were conscientious objectors.

One could have guessed that the quintessential "surfer band" of the 1960s was riding the Quaker wave. Consider such classic Beach Boys numbers as "God only Knows," "Good Vibrations" (good to quake to), and, of course, "Kokomo," which they claim is about a fictitious Caribbean island, but we know it is secretly about Kokomo, Indiana, founded in 1844 by the Quaker David Foster!

• • •

For further reading: Donald Swann, *Swann's Way: a Life in Song* (London: Arthur James, Ltd., 1993).

On being a–verse to music

When an American Quaker wakes up in England to the voice of a BBC radio presenter saying, "The next selection will be 'Dear Lord and Father of Mankind,'" he takes notice! Now, it must quickly be pointed out that hymns inspired by nineteenth century New England Quaker poets are not suddenly in heavy rotation on "Top of the Pops." This was BBC Radio 2's program "Good Morning Sunday," and the old favorite was being sung by the network's Dawn Chorus.

It is still rather remarkable, though, that the words of a nonconformist should be featured on a religious broadcast of the flagship cultural icon of Anglican Britannia! Even more unusual is that the poet, John Greenleaf Whittier (1807–1892), was a committed unprogrammed Friend all his life and staunchly opposed singing in Quaker worship. Yet many of his poems have been set to music and are counted among the Church's best–loved hymns. "Dear Lord and Father of Mankind" is excerpted from *The Brewing of Soma*; "Immortal Love, Forever Full" comes from *Our Master*; "O, Brother Man" is taken from *Worship*; and "This Still Room" is part of Whittier's classic *The Meeting*.

For much of his life, Whittier dedicated his poetry to the causes of antislavery and social reform, and he did not achieve widespread fame or fortune with his writing until after the American Civil War. His first major commercial success was his 1866 idyll, *Snowbound,* reminiscent of New England winters.

Ironically, Whittier's most well–loved hymn, "Dear Lord and Father of Mankind," is drawn from a poem blasting Christians for getting caught up in "sensual transports," of which he counted music as one! In *The Meeting* he writes, "I ask no organ's soulless breath," and in *Worship* he states his opposition to "dolorous chant." *Our Master* makes his claim to what Christian music ought to be:

> The heart must ring Thy Christian bells,
> Thy inward altars raise;
> Its faith and hope Thy canticles,
> And its obedience praise!

But that is okay; now that he is dead and buried, Whittier need not be conscience–stricken about the £50 royalty fee that goes to a songwriter each time the BBC plays the number!

• • •

For further reading: Elizabeth Gray Vining, *Mr. Whittier a Biography* (New York: The Viking Press, Inc., 1974).

Quakers get framed

Along with a testimony against music, early Friends also looked askance at art. Religious art was too closely connected with the "fallen" church, and dabbling in *easel* painting was seen as evidence that one had way too much leisure time. Better to engage in religious pursuits. Not many Friends were featured in art galleries during the first two hundred years. Hanging a Quaker had a very different connotation back then!

Times certainly have changed, though, as can be seen on the editorial page of the *Philadelphia Daily News*, where Pulitzer Prize–winning editorial cartoonist and Quaker, Signe Wilkinson, plies her syndicated trade. Active in her meeting, as a parent at Germantown Friends School, and with the Lucretia Mott Association, she maintains a busy association with Friends' concerns, along with her professional career.

A September 1998 cartoon of hers—seen by this writer in the *Times* of London—displays her keen political eye and an uncharacteristically good grasp of the Bible for a liberal Friend! With Monica Lewinsky's $2 million book deal on America's mind, Signe shows a preacher proclaiming in one panel, "The wages of sin is. . ." and in the next exclaiming dejectedly, "Oh, never mind," as a Monica caricature walks by fingering her loot.

One of the first artists with Quaker connections was Pennsylvania–born Benjamin West, who left America and Friends and became the historical painter for King George III, for whom he painted the famous *Death of Wolfe*. Had he remained a Quaker, it might have been

Death of Fox! But at least he did do the familiar mythical rendition of William Penn's "treaty" with the Indians.

Edward Hicks, the internationally known American "naive" painter of the early 1800s, was indulged in his many easel paintings of such scenes as the *Peaceable Kingdom,* not only because he earned his living as a sign and coach painter, but also because, as a recorded minister, his religious paintings were accepted as part of his ministry. And he was never paid during his lifetime the sums his paintings now fetch! In 1999, one of his *Peaceable Kingdom*s brought more than $4.5 million at Christie's auction house.

Home of Edward Hicks in Bucks County, Pennsylvania

Readers of *The Catholic Worker* have long been treated to the woodcuts of Fritz Eichenberg, also a Quaker. Born in Germany at the dawn of the twentieth century, he left that country in 1933, settled in the United States, and became a Friend in 1940, worshipping with Friends in Scarsdale, New York, and later Providence, Rhode Island. In addition to famous illustrations for various books, from Brontë and Tolstoy to Shakespeare, he also is the creator of Pendle Hill Quaker Study Center's familiar colophon.

Another artist who escaped Hitler's Germany was the Hungarian–born sculptor Peter Peri. Raised in a Jewish home under the name Laszlo Weisz, he left his homeland for Berlin, eventually leaving it, his religion, and his name behind and settling in London in the 1930s. He became a Friend in the 1950s, attending the Hampstead and Westminster meetings. His most widely recognized medium was colored concrete—proving that even convinced Friends prefer the concrete to the abstract!

Also a noted twentieth century Quaker sculptor, Sylvia Shaw Judson is best known for four pieces of public art: *The Little Gardener*, purchased by Jacqueline Kennedy for the White House Rose Garden, and three copies of *Mary Dyer*, one of four Quakers hanged (in the original sense of the word) in Boston in 1659–60. Judson's three Dyers are in Boston, near where the hangings occurred, in Philadelphia in front of the Friends Center, and on the campus of Earlham College

Statue of Mary Dyer at Earlham College (The blindfold is a student prank to prevent her witnessing the frolics of Earlham's "Olde English May Day.")

in Richmond, Indiana. Obviously out of sensitivity to the more conservative Midwestern Friends, Earlham's copy is truncated just below the knees—lest one catch a shocking glimpse of ankle!

We could mention many more artists—Edwin Bundy, Marcus Mote, Doyle Penrose, Walter West, Sandra Boynton, *et al.*—but we'll mention just one more: Joseph Southall (1861–1944), a Quaker–born pre–Raphaelite painter from Birmingham, England. Recognized for his revival of the Renaissance technique of tempera—yolk and wet plaster—he is a good one with whom to close. Given the success of Friendly artists such as Southall, we might say that the old opponents of the "frivolity" of art are left with egg on their faces!

Peter Peri sculpture, Quaker Meeting, *at Woodbrooke Quaker Centre*

• • •

For further reading: Eleanore Price Mather, *Edward Hicks. a Peaceable Season* (Princeton: The Pyne Press, 1973); Sylvia Shaw Judson, *The Quiet Eye* (London: Aurum Press, Ltd., 1982).

Heeding the call

Jim Casada, syndicated outdoors writer in the Greensboro *News & Record*, provided an unusual mention of Quakers in a 9 February 1997 article on coyote hunting. One might expect something about Friends in a column on *fox* hunting, but hardly in the same space as tracking furry animals—with guns—unless, of course, there were mention of the animal rights lobby among Quaker activists. But, indeed, there it was, right in the middle of Casada's story about a hunting trip to Oklahoma.

"My mentor [on the outing] was . . . an authority on predator hunting who is on the staff of Quaker Boy Game Calls." Later the writer also states, ". . . in areas such as North Carolina, [rabbit] calls such as Quaker Boy's Cottontail Screamer . . . work best."

A telephone conversation with Casada revealed the location of Quaker Boy Game Calls, and in a telephone call to their upstate New York offices, I learned that the name *Quaker* was used because there used to be Friends in the area. Today, however, there are none of that exotic species left in the vicinity—perhaps hunted into extinction? No Quakers are, in fact, connected with the Quaker Boy company.

The thought occurs, though, that a Quaker company concerned with "calls" would be very appropriate. It could help people in the process of discernment. Or perhaps closer to the big game business itself, could evangelical Friends lure heterodox Quakers to revivals with a Quaker Boy Hicksite Hooter? Could Universalist Friends appeal to the Inward Light of Christ–centered Quakers with a Quaker Boy Gurneyite Gobbler? Would pastoral Friends be able to trick Conservative Friends out from their "hedges" with a Quaker Boy Wilburite Whistler? The contest would probably be too close to *call*.

Beside ourselves with cloning

This essay comes from the "I know I'll never find another ewe" department. The 10 March 1997 *Newsweek* focused on the scientific and ethical issues raised by the successful cloning of Dolly, the Scottish sheep. Friends, of course, would be interested in such an issue, what with our penchant for ramming through pet concerns (sheep-ishly), early Friends' waging of the "Lamb's War," our notoriously woolly–headed thinking, and Quakers' fame for baaaaa–d puns. I won't even comment on our group worship of eighteenth century Quaker "saint" John *Wool*man! Whatever.

In an essay on the moral questions raised by Dolly's creation, *Newsweek* writer Kenneth Woodward quotes Quaker ethicist, James Childress, on the importance of consulting religious communities in the debate over cloning. Childress was cited because of his prominent work on the advisory panel established by President Clinton on the ethics of cloning. Childress was not quoted on his opinion about the ethics of Clinton's having pulled the wool over the nation's eyes in the Monica Lewinsky affair!

James Childress, raised in North Carolina Yearly Meeting's Surry Quarter, is a 1962 graduate of Guilford College who has gone on to a career as an author and educator in the field of ethics. He is co–editor of the standard reference work, *A New Dictionary of Christian Ethics*, and is a professor in the Department of Religious Studies and in the Medical College of the University of Virginia, where he enables many young people to earn their sheepskins.

• • •

For further reading: James Childress, *A Quaker Conscience* (Richmond, IN: Friends United Press, 1981).

With Friends like these...

Writing on 4 April 1997 about a recent trip to Chicago, *News & Record* columnist Rosemary Yardley described the fascination tourists to the Windy City have with the city's crime lore and such gangsters as Al Capone, Bugsy Moran, and John Dillinger. She didn't mention it in her article, but Dillinger also plays a small role in the Quaker lore of Chicago's neighboring state of Indiana.

John Dillinger (1903–1934) makes it into the *Dictionary of 20th Century Allusions*, which describes him as the first American to be named Public Enemy Number One. During the last nine years of his life he gained notoriety for a succession of robberies, murders, and prison escapes. In 1933 alone, he shot seventeen and killed ten—quite a career path for a boy who grew up attending the Friends meeting in Mooresville, Indiana! First day school teachers in Indiana are still terrorized by the story of how "little Johnny Dillinger" was expelled from his Sunday school class one day for acting up—*and went on to a life of crime*!

Dillinger met his end in 1934 when he was betrayed by his companion, Anna Sage, the infamous "woman in red," and was shot to death by FBI agents outside Chicago's Biograph Theater. If he had only spent more time attending meeting, he would have learned about the evils of those appearing in other–than–prescribed Quaker gray!

Also in the category of unlikely Friends is James Earl Huberty, son of a Quaker missionary to India and alumnus of Quaker Malone College in Ohio. He opened fire on a San Diego, California, McDonald's in the 1980s, killing more than twenty.

Unfortunately, we also can add Jim Jones, himself an entrant in the *Dictionary of Allusions* for leading more than nine hundred followers of his People's Temple to mass suicide at Jonestown, Guyana, in 1978. As a boy, he attended Sunday school at Bloomingport Friends Meeting outside Lynn, Indiana, before becoming a Disciples of Christ minister.

I wonder what it is about these Midwestern Quaker males that makes them dangerously aggressive? Wait a second—I was born and raised a Midwestern Quaker, and I'm not aggressive. *Dang it! I'm not!*

• • •

For further reading: John Toland, *The Dillinger Days* (New York: Random House, 1963).

Bloomingport (Indiana) Friends Meeting,
where a young Jim Jones attended Sunday school

Friends have gone to pot(tery)!

If you have ever wondered why Friends seem to have their fair share of crackpots, or why Quakers always seem to have "a full plate" (and I am not talking about dietary behavior at the typical meeting potluck/carry–in/pitch–in/covered dish/bring and share meal), a clue may be provided by the 24 April 1999 *News & Record* business section. A picture of Sarah Ferguson, Duchess of York, with Lord Wedgwood and the CEO of Wedgwood USA accompanies the notice of her agreement to act as spokeswoman for the upscale chinaware company.

Granted, the former wife of Prince Andrew has been known to act like she is "a couple of plates short of a full set." (Remember the toe–sucking pictures with a man other than her husband?) But the Duchess is not our Quaker connection here, no matter how rife York is with Quaker influence! Rather, it is the British porcelain industry itself.

William Cookworthy (what a great name to be associated with pottery), a devoutly plain eighteenth century Friend and apothecary from Devonshire, is the person who made possible England's preeminent position in porcelain manufacture. He discovered the Cornish deposits of clay that enabled him to develop ceramics of a quality equal to the Asian porcelain known as true "china."

Cookworthy founded the Plymouth Porcelain Company and in 1768 took out a patent on his chinaware process, his innovations earning him a reputation as the founder of the English china industry. His enterprise did not earn him much profit, however, and in 1774 he gave up the business to fellow Friend and partner, Richard Champion, who applied to Parliament the next year for an extension of the Cookworthy patent. But another Quaker, Josiah Wedgwood, backed by strong Straffordshire pottery interests and other forces in the House of Commons, succeeded in gaining the patents.

Champion was driven out of business and lived out the rest of his days in pursuit of Quaker interests, eventually removing to South Carolina, where he died. The Wedgwood dynasty, on the contrary, as can be seen in the photo with Sarah Ferguson and in the prices of Wedgwood china, most definitely did not "go South."

The ceramics section of the British Museum in London displays porcelain pieces by Cookworthy, Champion, and Wedgwood, evidence of their crucial contributions to British pottery. Their trials and foibles, though, point out that, no matter how important our achievements might be, we are still just "earthen vessels."

● ● ●

For further reading: Albert Douglas Selleck, *Cookworthy, 1705–80, and His Circle* (London: Baron Jay, Ltd., 1978).

Witness against the death penalty

Under the tantalizing headline, "A killer among the Quakers," Britain's *Independent Magazine* of 30 January 1999 reports on the case of Death Row prisoner Randolph Reeves, an Omahan Indian adopted in the 1950s by Nebraska Quakers Don and Barbara Reeves. Confessing to and convicted of murdering two women in the Lincoln (Nebraska) Friends meetinghouse in 1980 while in a drug–induced rage, Reeves faced execution on 14 January 1999, but he received a temporary stay of execution. The campaign against his execution was led by Friends who were directly affected by the murders, including the daughter of one of the women Reeves killed.

This case captured the attention of the United States and much of the Western world, in which the U.S. is the last remaining industrialized nation practicing capital punishment. In the United Kingdom, BBC radio and the print media gave attention to the case, in large part because of the anomaly of such violence occurring among peaceful Quakers and the absence of a spirit of vengeance in the Friends community.

Steve Lopez, a Philadelphia *Inquirer* journalist and reporter, once commented, while covering another difficult case involving Quakers, that people are amazed when Friends see in a crisis situation an opportunity to test their most cherished values, while others use such occasions to revert to Stone Age behavior!

Quaker opposition to capital punishment is legend, though seldom has it been demonstrated so dramatically. When William Penn became proprietor of Pennsylvania in the 1680s, he reduced the number of capital offenses in the colony from nearly two hundred to the two dictated by English law: treason and murder. Prison reformer Elizabeth Fry went even further, lobbying against all executions in England in the early 1800s and keeping vigil by the bedside of women in Newgate Gaol facing execution the next day.

Quaker efforts to end state–sanctioned murder were (and are) up against an appetite for blood, which can be sensed from a word that entered the English vocabulary from Fry's day. In the carnival–like atmosphere that pervaded public executions outside old Newgate, thousands would assemble to witness hangings on the permanent gallows. From this phenomenon we derive the joyous word "gala." And from the custom of sympathetic onlookers' hanging from the legs of victims to reduce their suffering by quicker strangulation, we get the word "hangers–on."

May Quakers and their "hangers–on" hasten the day when capital punishment itself meets a timely end.

• • •

For further reading: Arthur Koestler, *Reflections on Hanging* (New York: Macmillan, 1957).

"The Hanging Tree" pub near the site of
London's notorious Tyburn gallows in Hyde Park

Death in Friendswood

Almost as jarring as the headline "A killer among the Quakers" is the bold print in the 21 March 1999 edition of the *Independent*: "The day that death came calling at Friendswood." Almost as obvious as Quaker City, Ohio; Whittier, California; Earlham, Iowa; or even Plainfield, Indiana—here is a town name that screams out (silently, of course) Quaker! Although the article makes no mention of the Friends of Friendswood, Texas, there is, indeed, a connection.

Fortunately, the connection is not with the tragic story of thirty–two young women who, since 1971, have either vanished or been murdered along a stretch of I–45 near Friendswood. None of the cases has yet been solved. The mysterious killings are certainly out of character for a community once named the safest in America, where people routinely left their homes unlocked.

And it is out of character for the Quakers who founded the town in 1895. Leaving Kansas for the cheap and abundant farm land available in southeastern Texas, such pioneers as the Lewis and Brown families developed fig and orange orchards, grew rice and strawber-ries, started an academy, and established a Friends meeting open to the new evangelical principles arising out of the revivals that swept through Kansas after the Civil War.

Opposition to revivalism on the part of more traditional "slow" Friends is reputed to be one of the reasons for the migration. Town lore also has it that the Quakers came to Texas to offer a response and refuge to those being persecuted in a backlash against Reconstructionist policies in the former Confederate state. Before they moved away to the more economically enticing cities, ex–slaves were employed in Quaker farming operations.

It would be nice to think that such principled reasons were the basic motivation for settling Friendswood; in reality, it may have been primarily economics. In league with land developer John C. League, the early settlers subdivided their original tract of land, advertised in the national Quaker press, and sold off lots.

Such development continues. Friendswood's orchards and farms are now being replaced by the current agricultural crop of choice: housing developments with names like Quaker Village, Friends Crossing, and the Orchard. The Quaker school long ago evolved into the town's public school system. Friendswood has become a bedroom community for Houston, taking on, as the headline evokes, the problems that go along with such growth.

But the name remains, as does an active Friends church. Appropriate to the rapid growth of the town and the "fast" Friends who founded it, one of the more notable of former attenders at the Friendswood Friends Church was Hall of Fame fireballer Nolan Ryan, who worshipped there while a member of the Houston Astros baseball team. If ever Quakers decide that they want to salvage Friendswood's reputation as a Friendly sort of place, he would be the ideal person to make the *pitch*!

• • •

For further reading: Joycina Day Baker, *Friendswood, a Settlement of Friendly Folks* (Austin: Nortex Press, 1994).

Friendswood Friends Church

Some bare facts about Quakers

Novelist Bill Morris, at one time a reporter for the *News & Record,* wrote in the early 1990s about a visit to the Tiki Club, one of the "gentlemen's clubs" in High Point, North Carolina. He took special note of one "dancer" named Angel who "prances around without benefit of shirt." Morris asked her how she got her moniker, and she replied, "I am a Quaker; I don't smoke, drink alcohol or do drugs. That is why they call me Angel."

Before chagrined Friends rush to judgment, though, they should consider the history of Quakers' "going naked as a sign." Along with other nonconformist groups such as the Mennonites and Doukhabors, they were prone to follow in the steps of the biblical prophet, Isaiah, who was commanded of God to go naked "with buttocks uncovered" for three years through the streets of Jerusalem, as a sign of judgment against Egypt and Ethiopia (Isaiah 20:4).

One of the more eager of the early Friends to become a naturist for the Lord was Solomon Eccles, an eccentric seventeenth century convert to Quakerism. After his convincement he renounced his former career as a music teacher and sold his violins, but feeling guilty he bought them back and burned them—evidently an early example of the Friends testimony on *non–violins*!

In 1662, a day after a savage raid by the authorities on London's Bull and Mouth Meeting, Eccles protested the bloodshed and death that resulted from the raid by wandering naked through the nearby Smithfield market, with a pan of fire and brimstone on his head. On another occasion, Eccles went naked as a sign, once again with fire and brimstone on his head, to condemn a celebration of the Mass in Galway, Ireland.

Consistent with the prophet Isaiah's apocalyptic preachments, Eccles was happy to proclaim in word and in deed, "The end is in sight."

• • •

For further reading: Hugh Barbour, *The Quakers in Puritan England* (New Haven: Yale University Press, 1964).

Location of the Friends meeting held "at the sign of the Bull and Mouth" on London's Aldersgate Street

If the judge throws a fit, the jury will still acquit

During the first weekend of October 1995, much of America (if not the world) was fixated on the O. J. Simpson trial—the judicial process that was "the trial of the century" until Clinton's impeachment earned that title. When the jury in the Simpson murder case heeded defense attorney Johnny Cochran's plea, "If the glove doesn't fit, you must acquit," and returned a verdict of not guilty, many were surprised, feeling that Simpson had been shown clearly to have committed a double murder.

Many media references were made to the stunning jury decision, with some experts linking it to the legal concept of "jury nullification," a term that describes a jury's ignoring the law and "voting from the heart." The origin of the concept dates to Bushell's Case, a landmark event in English jurisprudence and one intimately linked to Friends.

In 1670 the King and Parliament enacted a stringent new Conventicle Act in England to prohibit meetings of religious dissenters. Heavy fines were levied against those who "harbored" a conventicle or preached at one. Even stiffer fines were enforced on officials who refused to enforce the law.

Meetinghouses of Friends and other nonconformists were stripped and occupied by guards—and sometimes by clergymen reading the Book of Common Prayer. When such an action was taken against the Friends meeting at White Hart Court in London, the Quakers moved into adjacent Gracechurch Street (which Friends called "Gracious" Street) and held meeting there.

While William Penn and William Meade were preaching in Gracious Street that August, they were arrested and brought to trial. Indicted for riot, they were given a jury trial—not a provision under the Conventicle Act. After hearing the evidence, the jury deliberated and returned a verdict of "not guilty" for Meade, and one of "guilty of speaking in Gracious Street" for Penn—the latter being a non–offense!

The court recorder commanded the jury to return a proper verdict and locked them up without "meat, drink, fire and tobacco" to encourage them in their task. Although the jury remained locked up into November, they responded by finding *both* Penn and Meade not guilty. Eventually the jury was freed and English judges ruled that "no jury may be fined for its verdict." The precedent is known as Bushell's Case, after the jury's foreman.

See! Friends were just as responsible for O. J.'s acquittal as Cochran's rhetoric! So, when does our talk show and millions of dollars in endorsements follow?

• • •

For further reading: Mary Maples Dunn, *William Penn, Politics and Conscience* (Princeton University Press, 1967).

Corner of Gracechurch and Lombard Streets
near the site of the old "Gracious Street" Friends meeting

Yet another Quaker "Paine"

There are not that many busts and statues of Quakers in the United Kingdom. Among the few are banker and philanthropist, Samuel Gurney in east London; cabinet minister, John Bright, in the Houses of Parliament; miller and humanitarian, Joseph Sturge, in Birmingham; baking magnate, George Palmer, in Reading; and George Cadbury, in the chocolate town of Bournville. But if a campaign in England is successful, another figure with close ties to Friends will be added.

Bust of George Cadbury at the Bournville Friends Meeting

An article in the *Independent* of 31 January 1999 notes that sentiment is growing to honor "one of the most subversive figures in our history—Thomas Paine." Yes, that Tom Paine—the one who coined the phrase "United States of America," wrote the famous words, "These are the times that try men's souls," and added rhetorical fire to the French Revolution. Hardly the stuff of Quaker reform, biscuits, and cocoa, but significant nonetheless!

The author of such seminal works as *Common Sense*, *Crisis*, and *The Rights of Man* was born to a Quaker father and Church of England mother in Thetford, England, in 1737. Although Tom was later confirmed as an Anglican, his father remained a Friend until his death; and Tom often noted that his democratic and anti–hierarchical beliefs were greatly influenced by Quaker principles.

Throughout his life, Paine seemed to be drawn into Quaker circles—often rather unorthodox ones. As an excise officer in Sussex, he lodged with a Quaker tobacconist and married his daughter, Elizabeth Ollive, in 1771. Removing to Philadelphia in 1774, he wrote *Common Sense* in defense of the colonies' complaint against George III, inveighing in one edition against

Statue of George Palmer in Palmer Park, Reading

Quaker passivity in the face of the King's tyranny. He repeated the criticism of Friends in subsequent issues of the paper, at one point urging that Quakers be heavily taxed to compensate for their inaction in the revolt.

Joining the Revolutionary army in 1776, Paine became aide–de–camp to fellow ex–Quaker General Nathanael Greene. After leaving the army, he worked as a clerk for another "fighting" Quaker—Philadelphia clockmaker, Owen Biddle. Unlike Paine, though, Biddle rejoined Friends after the war and became one of the founders of Westtown School.

Back in England in 1787, Paine dedicated his energies to building an iron bridge on the model of one he had planned in New Jersey. Once again, he was intersecting interests of Friends (remember the Darbys?)—although he still did not *bridge* the gap between his increasingly rationalist beliefs and the Society of Friends.

For all this and more, not only do some want to erect a statue in Paine's honor, but Richard Attenborough, the great film director, hopes to make a movie of his life. Attenborough's last great film,

Gandhi, featured a Quaker, Ben Kingsley, in the starring role. Why not follow up with a film *about* a (kind of) Quaker?

Not bad for the son of a simple English Quaker corsetmaker! Just imagine how history might have been different if Tom Paine had grown up to be *straightlaced*!

• • •

For further reading: David Freeman Hawke, *Paine* (San Francisco: Harper & Row, 1974).

Quaker forerunners of feminism

It looked to be the ideal place to find several references to Friends in print: the Manchester *Guardian*'s 25 January 1999 *G2* magazine published the results of a "Women of the Millennium" poll. Surely with Friends' record on gender equality there would be a number of Quakers on the list. But none ranked in the top ten, and in the accompanying article no Friends were even mentioned among the other vote getters. Dolly Parton even got votes (probably two), but the likes of Lucretia Mott, Elizabeth Fry, and Susan B. Anthony were missing. Not to be dissuaded, however, we can make a connection between one of the outstanding Quaker women of the twentieth century and number three on the *G2* list—the Pankhurst sisters.

Alice Paul, a Hicksite Friend from Moorestown, New Jersey, received a fellowship to study at Woodbrooke, a Quaker study centre in Birmingham, England, after graduating from Swarthmore College. While in Birmingham in 1909, she heard the woman's rights advocate Christabel Pankhurst give a speech. Her anger aroused by the loud boos that drowned out Pankhurst, Paul soon found herself marching in women's suffrage processions in London and shortly thereafter being thrown in prison for her part in a deputation that confronted the prime minister in Parliament—the first of numerous arrests that followed, some for throwing bricks at windows.

Back in the United States, Paul was greeted by a cold reception among Friends who were concerned about her involvement with violence. Responding to a query about whether she had, in fact, broken windows as reported, Paul said proudly that she had broken forty–

eight! People who follow their consciences can sometimes be a *pane*!

Finding Quaker inaction disappointing, she moved away from Friends while retaining membership and a self–identity as a Quaker. Adopting many of the strategies of the Pankhursts, and adding her own commitment to nonviolent protest and acceptance of suffering, Paul organized marches on Washington, D.C., hunger strikes, and picketing in front of the White House. In 1920 she saw these efforts rewarded by the passage of the constitutional amendment giving women the right to vote.

With that victory won, Paul authored in 1923 an equal rights amendment to protect working women, which she called "The Lucretia Mott Amendment." Finally passing a vote in Congress in 1972, it failed to win the necessary approval of two–thirds of the states.

Interviewed in the 23 March 1970 *Newsweek* at the age of 91, Alice Paul was quoted as saying, "When you put your hand to the plow, you can't put it down until you reach the end of the row." Perhaps Friends should *raise a row* over Alice Paul's exclusion from the Millennium list!

• • •

For further reading: Margaret Hope Bacon, *Mothers of Feminism* (San Francisco: Harper & Row, 1986).

What Quaker is on
the U.S. dollar?

Lucretia Mott was not the only Friend to have a proposed constitutional amendment named after her. A contemporary of hers, Susan B. Anthony, was also accorded that honor—and for a similar purpose: equal rights for women, but more about that later. Anthony's significance is recalled in a brief line from an article in Britain's *Independent* of 14 February 1999, about Hillary Rodham Clinton's possible designs on a New York Senate seat. The article referred to a recent speech the First Lady gave in front of thousands in upstate New York on "the centennial of the early feminist, Susan B. Anthony."

What manner of centennial it might have been escapes me. Anthony's years were 1820–1906! My guess, though, is that it was probably an anniversary of *something* radical—even if she would have been in her late seventies at the time.

Born to a Baptist mother and Quaker father, Anthony was raised according to Friends testimonies and joined a Hicksite Friends meeting when her family moved to Rochester, New York. She remained in membership all her life and always cited her Quaker upbringing, but, as her own views became more radical than many Friends felt comfortable with, she grew disaffected to the point that she was identified as a Unitarian in her later life.

Not that she started out so out–of–the–ordinary. Until the 1850s, Anthony was a school teacher whose extracurricular activities were involvement with the temperance movement and antislavery concerns. As she began organizing public occasions for these issues, however, and ran into opposition to women speaking in public and not staying "feminine," her efforts turned eventually to agitation for woman's rights.

Anthony served in the leadership of the National Woman Suffrage Association for more than thirty years and in 1872 was arrested and fined $100 for having "knowingly, wrongfully, and unlawfully voted for a representative to the Congress of the United States." She refused to pay the fine, and the judge refused to jail her, fearing she would use the incarceration to push her cause legally.

In 1878 she persuaded a sympathetic congressman to introduce an amendment to the Constitution allowing women the vote. It was thereafter known as the Susan B. Anthony amendment.

For her efforts, and to get an "other–than–male" on U.S. money, Anthony's profile was put on the ill–fated silver dollar, which is now scheduled to be replaced in the new century. That would probably not have phased Susan B., though. She rarely gave *currency* to the silliness of the times!

A feminist long before the word was popularized, Anthony was even one of the first to adopt a new, liberating costume for women designed by Amelia Bloomer. As always, Susan B. wore the trousers in the Quaker family!

• • •

For further reading: Lynn Sherr, *Failure Is Impossible: Susan B. Anthony in Her Own Words* (New York: Times Books, 1995).

Anchors *away*

As reported in Britain's *Independent* of 30 January 1999, a Connecticut court awarded a judgment of $8 million to former TV news presenter, Janet Peckinpaugh, because the WFSB station had dropped her in an action the jury interpreted as evidence of sex discrimination. The court was convinced that highly paid and veteran newscaster Peckinpaugh had been deemed by the TV station to be "on the wrong side of forty," and that this was the primary reason she had been dropped from her prime–time news spots in favor of younger women and eventually did not have her contract renewed.

An affiliate of U.S. television network CBS, WFSB should have known better! Another CBS affiliate in Philadelphia had experienced a similar controversy in the early 1990s, an episode involving Moorestown (New Jersey) Friends Meeting member, Diane Allen.

Like Peckinpaugh—blonde, professional, and over 40—Allen saw her role as co–anchor of WCAU Channel 10's nightly news reduced and eventually eliminated while younger women were being hired. Although she had been a popular Philadelphia area broadcaster for many years, she was reassigned to minor reporting duties; even these, Allen claimed, often seemed to be sabotaged by station management to make her job more difficult.

Refusing to go quietly, Allen accused the network of discrimination, eventually reaching a settlement with the station. She realized her accusation would end her broadcasting career, but she credited her Quaker sensitivities for finding the strength to push the case, as an example for women in the profession who would come after her.

Fellow Moorestown Quaker, Alice Paul, would have been proud! Allen went on to an equally successful career as an independent documentary film producer and was elected to a seat in the New Jersey Assembly where, probably, she was one of the younger members!

Reflecting on her landmark case—one of the first such discrimination actions in network broadcasting history—and on the sexism in the industry, Allen sums up her "sacking" with this great Quaker quip: "Watch out when your age exceeds your bra size!"

The "dreamer" had to have a "schemer!"

On one occasion at Woodbrooke, the Quaker Studies tutor asked students to respond to the question, "Who is a Quaker?" One response was, "Old, rich white people."

An exception that comes close to proving the rule is Bayard Rustin. A 2 March 1997 *News & Record* review of a biography of his life recounts the contributions of this African American, about whom the reviewer says, "None exerted a greater nor more beneficial impact on racial progress in our time. . . ."

Rustin, long a ghost writer for Martin Luther King, Jr., was King's strategist and adviser during the Montgomery, Alabama, bus boycott, the 1950s action that propelled King and Rosa Parks into the national spotlight. Additionally, Rustin is generally credited with being the guiding force in mobilizing the watershed 1963 March on Washington, made famous by King's "I have a dream" speech.

There should be a march on the *News & Record* editorial offices for not mentioning in the review that Rustin was also a Quaker! Moreover, along with his considerable Quaker commitments and publications, Rustin was active in the Fellowship of Reconciliation and the War Resisters League.

Rustin's education at two historically black universities provides further Quaker connection, although we are reaching here! Wilberforce University in Ohio is named for the British parliamentarian and abolitionist, William Wilberforce, who, though not a Friend, was drawn into the antislavery movement by Thomas Clarkson, author of the classic, *A Portraiture of Quakerism,* and of a biography of William Penn. Rustin's other college, Cheyney State in Pennsylvania, was formerly the Institute for Colored Youth, a training center for black teachers. It traces its roots to the will of a Philadelphia Quaker silversmith, Richard Humphreys, who in 1732 left money to establish a school for boys of African descent.

Rustin benefited much later from pioneering Quaker educational work; Richard Allen, founder of the African Methodist Episcopal Church, was a more direct beneficiary, receiving schooling from Philadelphia Quaker Anthony Benezet. Benezet had opened a night school for black children which he operated for many years during the eighteenth century in his own home at his own expense.

If only we could claim the AME Church as a Quaker spin–off, we could give a better retort to our aforementioned "whites only" skeptic than the standard reply, "Yes, but there are Kenyan Friends!"

• • •

For further reading: Jarvis Anderson, *Bayard Rustin: Troubles I've Seen* (New York: Harper Collins, 1997).

"Spelling" the potato
famine correctly

On St. Patrick's Day 1996, the A&E Network presented a documentary on the devastating Irish potato famine of the 1840s. The terrible suffering brought on by two successive years' failure of the potato crop led to the emigration of millions of Irish to the United States, many settling in Boston. Those immigrants' descendants would much later thrill to the success of the Boston Celtics' green–clad basketball team, one of whose star players in the 1970s and 1980s was M. L. Carr, a Guilford College graduate. But that is a very dubious Quaker connection! Fortunately, a far more profound one exists.

In contrast to the scathing indictment of Protestant groups who used the Irish tragedy to try to convert Catholics, Quakers were praised by the A&E program for their response to the famine. While other Christian groups set up soup kitchens and fed the starving on the condition that they convert, Friends offered food with no religious strings attached. Additionally, the Quaker Central Relief Committee distributed turnip seeds, provided means for fishing, and developed employment opportunities.

After the famine subsided, the committee published a ground–breaking study on the fundamental economic causes of poverty in Ireland, forming public opinion and government policy for years to come. As with their work to repeal the Corn Laws that prevented cheap grain from being imported, Quaker labors resulted in saving countless people from starvation.

A young U.S. Friend, who spent the summer of 1995 working in Ireland, learned how the reputation of Friends is still honored in that country. Upon learning that the American was a Quaker, an Irish woman exclaimed, "Ah, Quakers! You don't spit in *their* soup!" In defiance of other sects' use of soup as a "weapon" of compulsion during the famine, some Catholics spat in the soup they nonetheless needed for survival. But not in the Quakers' offerings.

And that's no small potatoes!

• • •

For further reading: Rob Goodbody, *A Suitable Channel: Quaker Relief in the Great Famine* (Ireland: Pale Publishing, 1995).

Mummy dearest

"Egyptian mummy found buried in garden," so proclaimed the headline in Britain's *Independent* of 15 February 1999. Not the sort of thing that would rivet the attention of a Quaker, unless that Friend were interested in alternative composting for organic vegetable beds. Further into the article, however, the Quaker confectionery connoisseur is drawn to this sentence: "The mummy was brought back to Britain in 1904 by the explorer John Wilhelm Rowntree, of the chocolate and cocoa family." The article goes on to add that Rowntree was dead within the year, at the age of thirty–seven—supposedly struck down by the "curse" of the mummy.

Actually, it was a fatal bout of pneumonia, contracted on a voyage to America in 1905. But frightened by the mummy which had been on display in the library of the Rowntrees' home, Low Hall in Scalby, North Yorkshire, the grieving family hastily buried it in the kitchen gardens. The incident was largely forgotten as the home passed out of family hands and became the offices of the National Union of Mineworkers. When the superintendent of the building and grounds was preparing a history of the old estate, a surviving daughter, Jean Rowntree, told him of the remains.

That solved a puzzle for the superintendent, who recalled having seen a mysterious blue, diamond–shaped light in the garden several times over the years. Though an old miner himself, he told the paper that he would not be doing any digging for the mummy; he was convinced of the potency of the "curse."

Another puzzle, though, is how the writer of the article could describe John Wilhelm Rowntree as an "explorer" and not as a pivotal Quaker figure!

Rowntree is described in Quaker histories as a leading light (blue, diamond–shaped?) for a group of scholarly and enthusiastic young Friends who sought to modernize the Religious Society at the end of the nineteenth century. At the age of twenty–seven, he delivered a riveting address at the influential 1895 Manchester Conference of Friends. Two years later, he developed plans with his close American friend, Rufus Jones, to publish a series of Quaker historical books. After Rowntree's untimely death, the project was carried out by Jones, William C. Braithwaite, and other Friends, and it became known as "The Rowntree Series."

John Wilhelm also wrote a plan in 1899 for a permanent "settlement" for religious study, a proposal realized in 1903 when Woodbrooke was established. Perhaps not wanting to be outdone by a rival chocolateer, George Cadbury donated his home and grounds to house the Quaker study centre.

Rowntree's Quakerly and philanthropic interests were typical of his family's activities. His grandfather, Joseph, helped establish the Quaker schools of Bootham and the Mount and the Friends Provident Institution. He also served on the Board of York's pioneering Quaker

Rowntree chocolate factory in York

mental hospital, the Retreat. An uncle, John Stephenson Rowntree, wrote a prize essay in 1859 that led Friends in Britain to end disownment for "marrying out" and to revise the Discipline to open Friends more to the world.

John Wilhelm's father, also named Joseph, turned the family grocery business into a thriving chocolate industry, using much of his subsequent wealth to endow a charitable trust, promote temperance, establish adult schools, and build a model housing development. A brother, Seebohm, wrote the seminal book, *Poverty — A Study in Town Life*, that led to significant change in public policy concerned with the poor.

And so, now we know why John Wilhelm Rowntree had a fascination for mummies: the Rowntrees were always trying to breathe life into dead or dying things.

• • •

For further reading: Joshua Rowntree, ed., *John Wilhelm Rowntree. Essays and Addresses* (London: Headley Bros., 1906).

You've got to have a sense of humor to be a Quaker!

The headline itself is enough to capture ones attention: "Virgin trip no joke for star of TV comedy" (the *Times* of London, 17 December 1998). Despite its proximity to Christmas, it wasn't about Mary's trip to Bethlehem, though. Nor was it about a first–time traveler. Rather, it referred to a trip on Richard Branson's notoriously ill–managed British train system, Virgin Rail, by the comedienne Victoria Wood.

Wood, a star performer and writer of the popular BBC series "Dinnerladies," took the train to the University of Manchester Institute of Science and Technology to receive an honorary degree. Her fame did not serve her well—she had to stand for two and one–half hours next to the train's first class toilet. Her stoic attitude about it all is enough to tip us off to her Quaker tendencies.

Wood, along with her husband and children, attends Hampstead Friends Meeting in London, a fact which dawned on this writer when I looked up from my meditations in the Hampstead meetinghouse during a visit to London in December 1998 and saw her familiar face in the row opposite! Her identity and regular attendance were confirmed by an elderly member of the meeting, who also noted that the meeting's clerk was an actress as well and had recently been on "Dinnerladies" herself in a non–recurring role. I guess when that meeting talks about an "acting clerk" it means it!

In an interview about her career, Wood once commented that it would be almost impossible to cope with the craziness of her professional life without her attendance at silent Quaker meeting. But she obviously was not quite sure whether Friends would give her famous persona "space" when she first visited Hampstead Meeting. As is the custom among British Friends, visitors are often asked to introduce themselves at the close of meeting for worship. Hesitantly, Wood rose and simply said, "Hello, I am Victoria."

With that introduction, a Friend in the room leaned over to her neighbor and whispered, "If I looked that much like Victoria Wood, I'd change my first name!"

• • •

For further reading: Victoria Wood, *Up to You. Porky* (London: Methuen, Ltd., 1985).

A shot in the dark

An ad in a March 1997 "TV Times" of the *News & Record* promoting the made–for–television movie, *A Prayer in the Dark,* contained this disclaimer: "*Warning*: Extremely Non–violent Scenes!" Text for the advertisement stated that the USA Network movie portrayed ". . . a Quaker whose devotion to nonviolence is tested when her family is taken hostage."

Some snooping about revealed that the movie was based on the novel, *Stronghold*, written by the late Stanley Ellin, a member of Brooklyn Friends Meeting. In spite of this Quaker pedigree, however, viewers of the film were treated to such scenes as Friends meeting for worship in a room in which unused chairs hung on Shaker pegboard. Hah! As if Friends ever have empty chairs in their meetinghouses!

The star of the movie, playing the role of "Quaker woman," was former TV "Wonder Woman," Lynda Carter, whose early acting expertise consisted largely (and we mean that literally) of amply filling her very skimpy costume. In spite of her old Quaker surname, though, she unfortunately is not related to this writer. We aren't even—ahem— *bosom buddies*.

A TV actress who *is* a Quaker is Kathy Baker, one of the ensemble cast of the popular 1990s U.S. show "Picket Fences," in which she played a small town doctor. According to a 30 March 1997 *New York Times* article on her, she was ". . . born in Midland, Texas, into a Quaker household that upheld the religion's principles of non-violence and good will."

The article goes on to quote her as saying she felt guilty about her success—about her nice house and her ability to take her children on skiing vacations and to buy her husband a pickup truck. Sounds Quaker to me: seek to do good, and do *well*, and then feel guilty about it!

Would that she could assuage some of that Quaker guilt by large donations to a certain Quaker college I know that also dwells in Dixie!

Friends on the silver screen

A piece in London's *Sunday Times Magazine* of 8 November 1998, on the release of DreamWorks' animated life of Moses, *The Prince of Egypt*, gives us opportunity to celebrate Quakers and film. Not that any Quakers are involved in Katzenberg/Geffen/Spielberg's DreamWorks or in biblical Egypt (and certainly Quakers cannot be accused of being *animated*). Instead, the article includes this line, barked out by Jeffrey Katzenberg to those planning the film project: "It's got to look like its drawn by Gustave Doré, painted by Monet and shot by David Lean."

Sir David Lean, legendary director of the classics *Dr. Zhivago* and *Lawrence of Arabia*, was raised in a strict Quaker home in Britain—one in which he wasn't even allowed to attend the cinema. Guess he showed his parents!

Since those anti–movie days, a surprising number of Friends have distinguished themselves on the silver screen: Indiana Quaker boy James Dean (*Rebel without a Cause*) and Brooklyn Friend F. Murray Abraham (*Amadeus*) come to mind. One could add plenty to the list if all those connected cinematically with Kevin Bacon (see essay #1) are included.

The Friend who received the most media attention in Britain during the autumn and winter of 1998–99 was Dame Judi Dench, a graduate of the Quaker boarding school, the Mount, and readily identified even in professional circles as a Friend. Hardly a week went by when she wasn't featured in the magazines and newspapers or on TV for her West End play, *Filumena,* and her role as Queen Elizabeth in *Shakespeare in Love*. The British papers were filled with pictures of Dench in March 1999, when the film won a best–picture Oscar, and she won the Academy Award as best supporting actress. Quakers weren't on the list of those thanked by Dench during her acceptance speech, but Friends can thank her for appearing in an appropriately modest dress!

One of the media mentions of Dench's film career worthy of noting is the *Times Magazine* of 31 October 1998, in which it was reported that she would be co–starring with Cher in *Tea with Mussolini*. Sounds like a valid enough argument for why Friends should have kept that ban on the cinema after all!

• • •

For further reading: Val Holley, *James Dean: The Biography* (New York: St. Martin's Press, 1995).

More Quakers at the movies

High Noon to most Friends stands for the outer limits of their patience in Sunday morning meeting for worship. By then the preacher had better stop talking (in the pastoral tradition), or the Spirit had better stop moving (in the unprogrammed tradition). But in the history of the cinema *High Noon* is a classic 1952 Western—one in which Quakerism plays a minor role.

A January 1999 *Radio Times* review by Barry Norman of the film, to be shown that week on BBC 2, makes mention of the part of the young Quaker bride played by then Hollywood star Grace Kelly. Her husband in the film, played by Gary Cooper, has to decide—against properly Quaker protestations—not "to get outta town" but to face three badmen scheduled to arrive on the noon train. I will not give away the ending, in deference to those whose Friends meetings have only recently allowed them to go to the movies, but I will reveal more of the subplot.

According to Barry Norman, the film's screenwriter (Carl Foreman) saw the saga as an allegory of the political situation in America in the early 1950s. Cooper's marshal stood for classic American liberalism, facing down the "badmen" of the virulently anti–Communist McCarthyites, while most Americans stood idly by. No less a light than John Wayne seems to confirm this. He called the film "the most un–American thing I've ever seen in my whole life."

We could connect this with Quakers by noting that Richard Nixon ascended to high office on an anti–Communist platform. Or we could note that, in one of the most celebrated anti–Communist cases of the era, antagonists Whittaker Chambers and Alger Hiss had Quaker connections: Chambers was a Friend, and Hiss was often mistaken for one, as he and his wife, Priscilla, a Bryn Mawr graduate, used Quaker plain speech. But, no, these are too obvious! We go for greater subtlety here. Instead, we will link the film with Cooper and Wayne themselves, neither of whom could ever be accused of being Quaker.

My suspicion is that Wayne actually hated *High Noon* for another reason: *he* had been first to define the role of the gunslinger love interest to a Quaker maid in his 1948 *Angel and the Badman*. Cooper, of course, was so taken by the exotica of Quaker wives that he went on to star as husband to Dorothy McGuire's Eliza Birdwell in the 1956 classic, *Friendly Persuasion.*

• • •

For further reading: Jessamyn West, *To See the Dream* (New York: Harcourt, Brace, 1957).

*Proof that Quakers are in the movies! Quaker Cinema
is located in Greensboro, North Carolina—
and appropriate to Quaker simplicity, it's cheap, too.*

Not by the hair of my chinny–chin–chin!

Among the questions Friends are often asked, especially those who remain hirsute from their flirtation with 1960s protest, is "Do Quakers have to wear a beard?" The easy answer, of course, is to respond with, "No, those are the Amish!" And besides, one might add, we are different from the Amish; they drive their own buggy; Quakers drive *others* buggy!

With Friends, though, it is never that simple, as the following article in the *News & Record* from the summer of 1995 displays.

In a piece about the Northeast United States traveling Circus Amok, performer Jennifer Miller is described as a juggler, stilt-walker, and clown. She is also the circus's "bearded lady." Her long, flowing facial hair is genuine.

Jennifer responded to questions about her distinctive chin decoration by saying that she was comfortable with her appearance. The article went on to say, "Both her parents were Jewish, but she was reared a practicing Quaker. Historically, Quakers have often taken stubborn, independent positions. In the Quaker tradition, personal appearance doesn't matter. It is each person's inner light that counts."

Hmmmm; that bit about stubborn Quakers rings a bell. Maybe that is why we Friends seem to have so many *hairy* issues in our meetings.

One difficult issue with which Jennifer might help our Quaker colleges is the question of alcohol use on campus. Increasingly, students at the historically Quaker schools are instigating for more liberal allowances for beverage consumption, especially at the colleges's "spring flings" such as Guilford's "Serendipity." At Guilford some students have pushed for a Bavarian–style "Oktoberfest" at the festival.

With Circus Amok and Jennifer Miller's Quaker sensitivities we might have the perfect Friendly compromise solution: the circus could provide the entertainment—and Jennifer could be the *beard* garden!